THE PSYCHOLOGICAL IMPACT OF CHRISTIANITY ON SOCIETY

Dr. Rushayne Stewart
Emmanuel Chigbu

Rushayne Stewart

CONTENTS

INTRODUCTION

Christianity has been one of the most influential forces in shaping societies across history. Its presence is evident not only in places of worship but also in moral frameworks, social institutions, and collective norms that continue to shape how people understand themselves and one another.

This book explores the psychological impact of Christianity on society. Rather than focusing solely on doctrine, it examines how belief functions socially, how it shapes identity, regulates behavior, creates belonging, and establishes boundaries. Social psychology provides the lens through which these dynamics are explored.

The discussion spans history, culture, and contemporary life, engaging with both the positive contributions of Christianity and the tensions, exclusions, and psychological costs that have accompanied its influence. The aim is not resolution, but clarity.

This work is written for a wide audience, students and educators, faith leaders and practitioners, and readers outside formal religious spaces. No specialized background is required, only a willingness to reflect honestly on how belief systems shape human experience.

ACKNOWLEDGMENTS

First of all, we return all glory to God Almighty for granting us the strength, wisdom, and knowledge to complete this book. Our special thanks also goes to our families who were our source of encouragements throughout the whole writing process.

Equally, we are grateful to all our lecturers who took out their time in teaching us during our schooling days. Of no doubt, this work was shaped by class discussions, conversations, scholarship, lived experience, and the courage of those who speak honestly about faith, identity, and belonging.

Finally, our sincere gratitude is extended to mentors, colleagues, students, and readers who continue to challenge easy answers and invite deeper reflection.

FOREWORD

Christianity has shaped societies not only through belief but also through behavior, institutions, and a shared moral imagination. *The Psychological Impact of Christianity on Society* delve into this intricate connection, examining how Christian beliefs and institutions influence social norms, identity formation, and psychological well-being of individuals. Its influence extends into law, education, family life, and social expectations, often in ways that are both psychological and cultural.

This book approaches Christianity as a lived social reality rather than a purely theological system. Drawing from social psychology, history, and cultural analysis, the authors explore how faith shapes identity, belonging, power, and meaning across time and context. The chapters that follow do not seek to defend or dismantle belief. They seek understanding. By holding together Christianity's constructive contributions and its psychological consequences, this work invites honest reflection across disciplines, convictions, and lived experience.

Throughout the books, reflective pauses are included to encourage the reader to delve into these issues, considering the ramifications on both individual and communal living. This is not an abstract process, but one that can be related to on a very real level by those seeking to understand the interplay between faith and society.

Finally, as you begin this journey through the pages that follow, may you find within them the enlightenment you seek regarding the psychological landscape that Christianity creates, a landscape that is both challenging and filled with great opportunity.

Rushayne Stewart,

PhD-CP & PhD-CE

CHAPTER ONE

CHRISTIANITY AND SOCIAL PSYCHOLOGY

C hristianity has shaped societies in ways that are both visible and deeply personal. Its influence can be seen in laws, customs, education, and family life, but it is also felt quietly within the human mind, shaping thoughts, emotions, identity, and a sense of belonging. To understand the psychological impact of Christianity on society, it is not enough to examine what the faith teaches. We must also explore how belief is lived, experienced, and shared.

This chapter begins that exploration by looking at Christianity through a social and psychological lens. Rather than focusing on doctrine or theology, it asks how faith operates within everyday life. How does belief shape the way people relate to one another? How does it influence identity, meaning, and moral direction? And how does it affect both the inner life of individuals and the shared life of communities?

Chapter One introduces Christianity as a social force that works through relationships, stories, and shared values. It explores how belief takes root in the social world, shapes the inner psychological life, and contributes to identity, belonging, and moral order. At the same time, it acknowledges that faith can unite and divide, offering comfort and meaning while also creating boundaries and tension.

By the end of this chapter, readers will have a framework for understanding Christianity not only as a religion, but as a powerful influence on human behavior and social life. This foundation prepares us to look more closely at how these psychological and social forces developed over time.

Faith And The Social World We Live In

Christianity is more than a set of beliefs held quietly in the mind. It is lived out in families, communities, traditions, and everyday relationships. For centuries, it has shaped how people gather, how they understand right and wrong, and how they relate to one another. Whether through worship, moral teachings, social expectations, or shared rituals, Christianity has played a visible and lasting role in shaping social life.

When people think about Christianity, they often focus on theology, what the faith teaches about God, salvation, and morality. Yet beneath those teachings lies something equally powerful: the way faith shapes human behavior, emotions, identity, and social bonds. Beliefs do not remain abstract ideas; they influence how people think, feel, and act within the world they share with others.

This is where social psychology enters the conversation. Social psychology helps us understand how belief systems shape how people interact within groups and societies. It explores how shared values shape behavior, how communities reinforce norms, and how individuals internalize expectations. Viewed through this lens, Christianity becomes not only a religious tradition but a powerful social force that shapes collective life.

Christianity has not only influenced individual lives; it has helped form communities, institutions, and cultures. Over time, it has shaped laws, educational systems, family structures, and moral norms. These influences did not remain confined to churches or religious spaces. They became part of everyday life, shaping how people understand responsibility, authority, and belonging.

People do not develop in isolation. From early life onward, a sense of self emerges through relationships, cultural influences, language, and shared experiences. Within this social environment, faith takes root and becomes part of everyday life. Early Christian communities were built around shared practices and mutual responsibility, reinforcing the idea that faith was meant to be lived in relationship with others rather than practiced alone.

Through shared beliefs and rituals, Christianity fostered a sense of belonging. These shared experiences helped individuals feel connected to something larger than themselves, especially during times of uncertainty or hardship. Faith communities often became spaces of support, offering meaning, comfort, and a sense of stability in an unpredictable world.

At the same time, social belonging carries expectations. Every community draws lines around acceptable behavior, shared values, and moral responsibility. Christianity contributed to these boundaries by shaping ideas about how people should live, relate to others, and conduct themselves. These expectations influenced daily behavior, family life, and social roles, quietly guiding conduct across generations.

As Christianity became woven into the fabric of society, its values extended beyond religious gatherings. Moral frameworks influenced laws, customs, and institutions, shaping social norms even among those who did not actively practice the faith. In this way, Christianity became part of the social atmosphere, present in expectations, traditions, and shared understandings. Additionally, the ethical teachings of Christianity fostered a sense of community and compassion, encouraging charitable actions and social responsibility. Concepts such as forgiveness, humility, and sacrifice permeated not only personal relationships but also institutional practices, promoting welfare systems and humanitarian efforts. Even among secular circles, the echoes of Christian ethics in debates on ethical dilemmas and social issues illustrate its lasting impact, revealing how deeply entrenched these beliefs have become in the collective consciousness.

Living within a faith-shaped social world affects the inner life as well. Belonging can bring comfort, purpose, and emotional security. Yet it can also bring pressure, fear of judgment, or inner conflict when individuals struggle to meet communal expectations. These psychological experiences reveal how closely social life and inner life are connected.

Faith and the social world are deeply intertwined. Christianity has functioned as both a unifying presence and a regulating force, shaping how people connect, behave, and find meaning. By viewing faith within its social context, we begin to understand how its psychological impact reaches far tremendously, into relationships, institutions, and the shared human experience that continues to shape society today.

The Social Side Of Being Human

Human beings are social by nature. From birth, identity is shaped through interaction, family, culture, language, and shared values, all of which contribute to how individuals come to understand who they are. Long before people are capable of choosing their own beliefs, they are already absorbing meaning from the social world around them. No belief exists in isolation, and no faith is practiced alone. Christianity, like all major belief systems, is experienced within a social context.

People learn who they are through relationships. Identity forms through connection, how one is spoken to, valued, corrected, and accepted. These early interactions shape not only personality, but moral understanding and emotional awareness. As individuals grow, they continue to be shaped by the groups they belong to, adopting shared norms and internalizing collective expectations.

Faith enters this social process naturally. Christianity has historically taken root not simply through ideas, but through community. Beliefs are learned through stories, rituals, and relationships, passed from generation to generation within families and social groups. In this way, faith becomes woven into everyday life, shaping how people understand themselves and others.

Churches, congregations, and faith communities have long served as spaces where people find belonging, support, and shared meaning. These spaces offer more than spiritual instruction; they provide structure to social life. Within them, people learn to relate to others, cooperate, forgive, and resolve conflict. Community life reinforces shared values and strengthens social bonds.

Through shared symbols, practices, and narratives, Christianity has helped shape collective identity. These shared elements create a sense of "we," offering members a common language and moral framework. This collective identity can foster unity, encouraging cooperation and mutual responsibility among group members.

At the same time, social life is shaped by expectations. Belonging often comes with rules, spoken and unspoken, about behavior, roles, and values. Christianity has historically contributed to these expectations, influencing how societies define morality, responsibility, and acceptable conduct. These expectations help maintain order, but they also define limits. Social norms are powerful because they are reinforced daily. Approval and disapproval, inclusion and exclusion, affirmation and correction all communicate what a community values. Over time, individuals internalize these messages, shaping behavior not only out of belief, but out of a desire to belong and be accepted.

This process highlights an important psychological reality: people are often influenced as much by social pressure as by personal conviction. Faith is not only believed; it is lived under the watchful presence of others. The desire to belong can deepen commitment, but it can also create tension when personal experience conflicts with communal expectations.

Understanding the social side of being human helps explain why Christianity has been so influential across cultures and centuries. Its power lies not only in doctrine but in its ability to organize social life, create shared meaning, and shape identity within the community. Faith becomes part of how people understand themselves in relation to others.

By recognizing this social foundation, we gain deeper insight into Christianity's psychological impact. The influence of faith unfolds within relationships, communities, and shared life. This understanding prepares us to explore how belief shapes the inner world of the mind, where identity, emotion, and meaning continue to take form.

The Psychological Life Beneath Belief

Behind every belief system lies the human mind. Faith does not exist only in outward practice or spoken confession; it reaches inward, shaping how people interpret their experiences, cope with hardship, and find meaning in life. Christianity, in particular, has long influenced the inner world, guiding how individuals understand suffering, hope, and purpose when life feels uncertain.

For many, Christianity has offered comfort in times of suffering and reassurance in moments of despair. In seasons of loss, fear, or confusion, faith has provided language for endurance and hope. These psychological effects are often deeply personal, shaping emotions such as guilt and forgiveness, fear and courage, despair, and resilience. Long before belief is articulated, it is often *felt*.

Belief shapes how people make sense of their lives. Christianity provides interpretive frameworks for understanding success and failure, joy, and pain, right and wrong. These frameworks influence how individuals assign meaning to events, helping them place individual experiences within a larger story that gives coherence to life.

Over time, belief also shapes emotional responses. Faith can influence how people respond to disappointment, how they recover from moral failure, and how they extend compassion to themselves and others. Emotional patterns are reinforced through teaching, ritual, and repetition, becoming part of the inner rhythm of daily life.

Christianity also influences how individuals see themselves. It shapes inner narratives; stories people tell themselves about who they are and what their lives mean. Some experience faith as affirming, viewing themselves as forgiven, valued, and purposeful. Others may internalize more critical narratives, seeing themselves as unworthy, condemned, or perpetually falling short. These inner stories play a powerful role in mental and emotional well-being.

Psychological influence, however, is not uniform. The same beliefs that bring comfort to one person may create tension for another. Faith is experienced through personal history, social context, and interpretation. What heals in one setting may wound in another, revealing the complexity of belief's psychological impact.

At times, belief offers strength and stability. It can encourage resilience, self-discipline, and hope in the face of adversity. Many people draw emotional strength from faith, finding motivation to endure hardship and to act with compassion even when circumstances are difficult.

At other times, belief can produce inner conflict. When individuals feel unable to meet moral or social expectations, faith may generate anxiety, shame, or fear of judgment. These experiences are often intensified when belief is closely tied to identity and belonging. The desire to be faithful can become a source of emotional strain rather than a source of comfort.

Exploring the psychological life beneath belief allows us to see both the healing and the strain that faith can bring. Christianity's influence on the mind is neither entirely positive nor entirely harmful; it is complex, shaped by context, community, and interpretation. Recognizing this complexity opens space for honest reflection rather than simple conclusions. By looking beneath outward expressions of faith, we gain a deeper understanding of how Christianity shapes the inner life. Belief influences thought patterns, emotional responses, and self-understanding in lasting ways. This inner formation prepares the ground for the next movement of the chapter, how belief moves outward again, shaping identity, behavior, and the social world people inhabit.

How Belief Shapes Identity

Identity is formed through stories, stories people tell about who they are, where they belong, and what their lives mean. These stories are shaped over time through family, culture, memory, and shared experience. Christianity has long provided such narratives, offering explanations about creation, purpose, morality, and destiny. Through these stories, individuals learn to see themselves and understand their place within the larger social world.

Faith-based narratives do more than explain life; they organize it. They offer a framework for understanding responsibility, meaning, and direction. Christianity has historically given people language to describe who they are, what they are called to do, and how they should live. These narratives often become deeply rooted, shaping identity in ways that feel natural and unquestioned.

Belonging to a faith community can strengthen this sense of identity. Shared beliefs, rituals, and values provide clarity about what matters and why. For many, faith offers direction during moments of uncertainty, helping individuals make decisions aligned with deeply held values. This sense of grounding can be a source of confidence and inner stability.

Identity shaped by faith often influences character. Christianity has encouraged qualities such as discipline, compassion, humility, and responsibility. These values are reinforced through teaching, community life, and moral example. Over time, they become part of how individuals understand themselves and how they choose to act in the world.

Faith can also provide a sense of purpose beyond the self. Identifying with something larger than personal ambition or circumstance often brings meaning and motivation. For many, this shared purpose strengthens resilience and fosters commitment to family, community, and service to others.

Yet identity formation is rarely simple or uniform. When belief systems define who belongs and who does not, identity can become a source of tension rather than comfort. Individuals who feel marginalized, excluded, or judged may struggle to reconcile personal experience with communal expectations. This conflict can quietly shape self-perception and emotional well-being.

For some, identity becomes fractured when personal realities do not align with prescribed roles or moral ideals. Navigating these tensions can produce inner conflict, uncertainty, or self-doubt. The desire to belong may clash with the need for authenticity, creating psychological strain that is often deeply personal and difficult to express.

These struggles are intensified when identity is closely tied to acceptance within a community. When belonging feels conditional, individuals may experience fear of rejection or pressure to conform. Such experiences highlight how powerfully social belonging influences identity and self-worth.

At the same time, identity is not static. It continues to evolve as people reflect, question, and reinterpret their experiences. Faith may be embraced, redefined, or challenged as individuals grow and encounter new perspectives. This process of reflection is part of the ongoing relationship between belief and identity.

Understanding how belief shapes identity helps us

see why faith exerts such enduring influence in human life. Identity lies at the intersection of inner experience and social expectation. As belief shapes both, it becomes a powerful force in shaping how individuals live, relate to one another, and understanding themselves, setting the stage for examining how meaning, order, and moral direction emerge within society.

Meaning, Order, And Moral Direction

One of Christianity's most enduring psychological influences lies in its ability to provide meaning. Across history, people have turned to faith to answer life's deepest questions: *Why am I here? How should I live? What gives life value?* In moments of joy and in times of suffering, Christianity has offered explanations that help individuals make sense of their experiences and locate themselves within a larger story.

Meaning is not only philosophical; it is deeply psychological. When life feels uncertain or painful, belief can offer reassurance that suffering is not random and that life has purpose beyond immediate circumstances. Christianity has provided many people with a sense of direction, helping them endure hardship by placing it within a moral and spiritual framework that offers hope and continuity.

This search for meaning extends beyond the individual. Shared beliefs create shared understandings about purpose and responsibility. Christianity has helped shape collective ideas about what matters, what is worth striving for, and how people ought to treat one another. These shared meanings become part of the social fabric, influencing how communities organize life together.

Out of shared meaning grows order. Societies depend on agreed-upon values to function, and Christianity has historically contributed to moral codes that guide behavior and relationships. Teachings about compassion, forgiveness, responsibility, and care for others have influenced family life, community interaction, and social cooperation. In this way, faith has played a role in stabilizing social life.

Moral direction provides guidance not only during moments of crisis, but in everyday decisions. It shapes how people approach honesty, conflict, work, and relationships. For many, Christianity has offered a moral compass to navigate the complexities of social life, encouraging behavior that fosters trust and mutual responsibility.

Yet moral systems do more than guide; they also define limits. As societies adopt shared values, boundaries emerge between what is acceptable and what is unacceptable. These boundaries help maintain order and clarity, but they also draw distinctions that can separate individuals and groups. Moral direction, therefore, always carries both protective and restrictive dimensions.

These boundaries can foster unity by reinforcing shared standards, but they can also become sources of tension. When moral expectations are rigidly applied, individuals who struggle to conform may feel judged, excluded, or misunderstood. The psychological impact of these experiences can be profound, affecting self-worth, a sense of belonging, and emotional well-being.

Understanding this dual role of faith, as a source of meaning and a system of moral order, is essential. Christianity's influence cannot be understood solely in terms of comfort or guidance; it must also be examined in terms of how moral expectations shape social life and personal experience. Meaning and order are deeply connected, and together they shape both stability and conflict.

For many, moral direction offers clarity and reassurance. For others, it introduces struggle and uncertainty. These differing experiences highlight how the same belief system can function differently depending on context, interpretation, and lived reality. Faith's psychological impact is therefore complex and layered.

By examining how Christianity provides meaning, establishes order, and defines moral direction, we gain insight into its powerful role in shaping society. This understanding prepares us to explore the next dimension of faith's influence, how unity and order can coexist with division and conflict, and how belief can both connect and separate people within the social world.

When Belief Unites And When It Divides

Christianity has long carried the power to unite people around shared belief and purpose. Across history, it has brought individuals together into communities marked by common values, mutual care, and moral responsibility. Faith has inspired acts of compassion, social reform, and service, motivating people to look beyond themselves and work for others' well-being.

Shared belief often strengthens social bonds. When people gather around common convictions, they develop a sense of trust and solidarity. Christianity has fostered this unity through shared worship, moral commitments, and collective identity. These shared elements help individuals feel connected, supported, and anchored within a larger social framework.

Faith has also played a role in motivating social change. Christian values have inspired movements centered on justice, care for the vulnerable, education, and community development. For many, belief has served as a moral call to action, encouraging responsibility toward others and engagement with the broader social world.

At the same time, unity has often come with boundaries. The same beliefs that draw people together can also create divisions. When faith is used to define who belongs and who does not, lines are drawn that separate communities, identities, and experiences. These divisions may be subtle or overt, but their psychological effects are deeply felt.

Conflict often arises when belief is enforced rigidly or elevated above compassion. Throughout history, Christianity has sometimes been used to justify inequality, exclusion, or dominance. In such moments, faith shifts from a source of connection to a mechanism of control, shaping social hierarchies and reinforcing power differences.

The psychological impact of this tension is complex. Faith can bring comfort and security, while simultaneously generating fear, anxiety, or resentment. Individuals may experience deep belonging within a community while also witnessing or experiencing exclusion.

These contradictions reflect the layered nature of belief as both a unifying and dividing force. For those included within the boundaries of belief, faith can affirm identity and worth. For those pushed to the margins, it can become a source of emotional strain, confusion, or pain. These experiences shape how individuals relate not only to faith, but also to themselves and to society at large.

Recognizing this complexity does not diminish the significance of Christianity. Rather, it allows for a more honest and humane understanding of its role in social life. Faith is not a single experience shared equally by all; it is lived differently in different contexts, through different interpretations, and from unusual positions within a community.

Understanding both the unifying and dividing effects of belief helps explain Christianity's enduring influence. Its power lies not only in what it teaches, but in how it organizes social life, shapes identity, and defines belonging. These forces operate simultaneously, producing outcomes that are both constructive and challenging.

This chapter has introduced Christianity as both a social and psychological force, one that shapes behavior, identity, meaning, and belonging. With this foundation in place, the chapters that follow will explore how these influences unfolded across history, how they contributed to both conflict and cohesion, and how they continue to shape lives and societies today.

Reflective Pause

✓ Faith shapes more than belief. It shapes how people understand themselves, relate to others, and find meaning in the world. As this chapter has shown, Christianity operates within both the social world and the inner life, influencing identity, emotion, belonging, and moral direction.

✓ For some, faith has been a source of comfort, clarity, and purpose. For others, it has raised questions, created tension, or drawn boundaries that feel difficult to navigate. These experiences are not abstract; they are lived, felt, and deeply human.

✓ Before moving forward, take a moment to reflect on how belief has shaped your own understanding of self, community, and meaning. Consider the ways faith can unite and divide, comfort, and challenge. This reflection is not about agreement or judgment, but awareness, recognizing the complex role belief plays in shaping human experience.

The Bridge

Understanding Christianity's psychological impact begins with recognizing how belief shapes the social world and the human mind. Yet these influences did not emerge overnight. They were formed, reinforced, and transformed across centuries of history, as Christianity moved from a small movement into a global institution.

The ways belief shapes identity, meaning, and social boundaries today are deeply connected to the faith's historical development. The structures of authority, moral expectations, and communal life explored in this chapter were shaped by specific historical moments, times of growth, conflict, adaptation, and transformation.

Chapter Two turns our attention to that history. It traces Christianity's journey from its early communal beginnings through its institutional formation and expansion across different eras. By exploring how the Church developed across changing social and political contexts, the next chapter reveals how historical conditions shaped faith's psychological influence on societies.

As we move forward, history becomes more than background; it becomes a lens for understanding why Christianity continues to shape behavior, belonging, and social order in the present. What follows is not simply a record of events, but a story of how belief, power, and social life became intertwined in ways that continue to affect the human experience today.

CHAPTER TWO

HISTORICAL AND INSTITUTIONAL DEVELOPMENT OF CHRISTIANITY

C hristianity did not begin as a powerful institution shaping nations and cultures. It began as a movement, small, vulnerable, and rooted in shared belief rather than formal structure. Yet over time, that movement grew, organized, adapted, and eventually became one of the most influential forces in human history. To understand the psychological impact of Christianity on society, it is essential to understand how this transformation unfolded.

The influence of faith on identity, behavior, and belonging explored in the previous chapter did not develop in isolation. It was shaped by historical moments, social pressures, and the gradual formation of institutions that carried belief forward across generations. As Christianity moved through different periods of history, it absorbed cultural influences, responded to political realities, and developed systems of authority that shaped both social life and inner experience.

This chapter traces that journey. It follows Christianity from its early communal beginnings to its emergence as an organized church, examining how structure, leadership, and authority took shape. Along the way, it explores how historical circumstances shaped the lived, understood, and enforced practices of faith within society. Each stage of development brought new opportunities for unity and meaning, as well as new tensions and challenges.

As Christianity became intertwined with political power, education, and social order, its psychological influence deepened. Belief was no longer only a personal or communal experience; it became embedded in laws, traditions, and everyday expectations. Faith began to shape not only what people believed, but how they behaved, obeyed, and understood their place within society.

This chapter does not aim to offer a simple timeline of events. Instead, it explores how history shaped the social and psychological role of Christianity. By examining the faith's institutional development across different eras, we gain insight into how belief systems evolve and how their influence on the human mind and social life becomes enduring.

What follows is a journey through time, not to glorify or condemn, but to understand. The historical development of Christianity provides the context needed to understand later chapters, where conflict, discrimination, contribution, culture, and social boundaries come into sharper focus. History, in this sense, is not distant; it is the foundation upon which present experiences are built.

From Movement To Community

Christianity began not as an institution, but as a

movement rooted in shared experience and belief. Its earliest followers were drawn together by a message that spoke to hope, meaning, and transformation. Without buildings, hierarchy, or formal power, the first Christian communities were formed through relationships, home gatherings, shared meals, collective prayer, and mutual care. Faith, in these early moments, was lived more than was organized.

Church historians reckon Early Christianity to begin with the ministry of Jesus (c. 27–30) and end with the First Council of Nicaea. It is typically divided into two periods: the Apostolic Age (c. 30–100, when the first apostles were still alive) and the Ante-Nicene Period (c. 100–325). The Apostolic Age is named after the Apostles and their missionary activities. (McCain, 2005) It holds special significance in Christian tradition as the age of the direct apostles of Jesus. A primary source for the Apostolic Age is the Acts of the Apostles, but its historical accuracy has been debated and its coverage is partial, focusing especially from Acts 15 onwards on the ministry of Paul, and ending around 62 AD with Paul preaching in Rome under house arrest. In the last century, scholars have come to appreciate Paul as the actual founder of the religious movement that would become Christianity. (Kanu, 2022)

These early communities were shaped by closeness and vulnerability. Believers depended on one another for support, encouragement, and survival.

In a world where Christianity was not widely accepted, belonging carried both emotional comfort and personal risk. This shared vulnerability strengthened bonds and created a powerful sense of identity rooted in trust and commitment. Community life became central to how belief was understood and practiced. Teachings were passed down through storytelling, memory, and shared interpretation rather than formal instruction. Belief was reinforced through participation in worship, service, and daily interaction. Faith grew not only through what was taught, but through what was lived together.

Psychologically, this communal structure played a significant role. Belonging offered reassurance in uncertain times, while shared belief helped individuals interpret hardship and persecution. The community became a space where meaning was affirmed, and identity was reinforced. In this way, early Christianity provided both emotional support and a framework for understanding suffering.

As the movement spread, diversity increased. New communities formed across different regions, cultures, and social groups. While this expansion strengthened Christianity's reach, it also introduced challenges. Differences in custom, language, and interpretation required negotiation and adaptation. Community life now involved balancing unity with diversity, shared belief with varied experience.

These growing communities began to develop informal leadership and shared practices. Certain individuals emerged as guides, teachers, or caretakers, helping maintain order and continuity. While still far from institutional, these early structures marked the beginning of organization. They reflected a human need for stability, guidance, and shared direction within communal life.

At the same time, community boundaries became more defined. As belief took shape, distinctions between insiders and outsiders emerged. These boundaries helped protect group identity, but they also introduced tension. Belonging was no longer only about shared experience; it increasingly involved shared belief and commitment. This shift carried psychological weight, shaping how individuals understood loyalty, faithfulness, and responsibility.

The movement's growth also brought increased visibility, with its scrutiny and opposition. Communities learned to navigate fear, resilience, and solidarity under pressure. Persecution, rather than dissolving the movement, often strengthened internal bonds. Shared struggle reinforced collective identity and deepened emotional commitment to the faith.

From these early beginnings, Christianity moved steadily toward greater organization. What began as a movement of shared belief and lived community laid the groundwork for more formal structures. The psychological foundations formed here, belonging, meaning, identity, and resilience, would continue to shape Christianity as it evolved into an institution. This transition from movement to community set the stage for the next phase of development, where informal gatherings would gradually give way to structured leadership and institutional authority. It is to this process of foundation and organization that we now turn.

The Foundation Of The Church

As Christian communities grew in number and spread across regions, the need for structure became increasingly clear. What began as informal gatherings rooted in shared belief and mutual care could no longer function solely with closeness and familiarity. Communities needed continuity, guidance, and a way to preserve shared meaning across distance and time. Out of this need, the foundations of the Church began to take shape.

What exactly is Church? The word **"church,"** as we have seen from the Bible (Matt 16:18, Matt 18:17, Acts 2:47). It is an institution and the gathering of the community of God's people who have been called out of darkness to Christ's marvelous light (1 Peter 2:9). Both earthbound and heavenly Protestants are a part of the church, which is the universal, immaterial group of believers who have been set free by the blood of Christ. The Greek word for church is **ecclesia**, which simply means "called out." That refers to individuals who have responded to His call for salvation and come into the light. The church is not a gathering place for socializing.

It must be based on biblical and spiritual principles. In addition, the church is the temple of the Spirit, filled with the fullness of Christ and marked by God's presence. In order to participate in worship, communion, discipleship, fellowship, ministry, and outreach, the church regularly gathers as a covenant community.

Then, leadership emerged gradually, not first

as power, but as service. Certain individuals were responsible for teaching, organizing gatherings, and caring for the community's spiritual and practical needs. These roles helped maintain unity and consistency, especially as communities expanded and original witnesses were no longer present. Leadership provided reassurance and stability, helping believers feel anchored in a shared direction. With leadership came shared practices. Rituals such as communal worship, prayer, and remembrance became more formalized. These practices reinforced identity and belonging, giving members a sense of continuity and rhythm in their spiritual and social lives. Repetition strengthened memory, and memory strengthened belief. Over time, these shared practices became central to what they meant to belong.

The formation of the Church also involved defining belief. As Christianity spread into new cultural settings, interpretations varied. To preserve unity, communities began to articulate common understandings of faith. These shared beliefs helped protect collective identity, offering clarity about what the community stood for and how it understood itself within the wider world.

Psychologically, this structure provided security. Clear beliefs and shared authority reduced uncertainty and helped individuals feel grounded. Faith was no longer only a personal conviction; it became a shared framework that offered answers, guidance, and reassurance. For many, this brought comfort and a stronger sense of purpose. At the same time, the structure introduced hierarchy. As roles became defined, distinctions emerged between leaders and followers, teachers, and learners. Authority became a feature of religious life, shaping how obedience, loyalty, and trust were understood.

These dynamics influenced how individuals related not only to faith, but to one another within the community. The Church also became a moral guide.

Expectations about behavior, responsibility, and conduct were reinforced through teaching and communal accountability. These moral frameworks helped regulate social life, shaping families, relationships, and community standards. Belief now carried not only meaning, but expectation.

As the organization increased, so did visibility. The Church became more recognizable in society, attracting both supporters and critics. Its growing influence brought opportunities for expansion, but also heightened tension with surrounding authorities and cultures. This visibility would soon place the Church in direct conflict with existing social and political powers. Despite these challenges, institutional foundations allowed Christianity to endure. Structure-preserved belief across generations, enabling the faith to survive loss, persecution, and change. The Church became a vessel through which belief was carried forward, shaping both inner life and social order.

The foundation of the Church marked a turning point. Christianity was no longer only a movement of shared experience; it was becoming an institution with authority, influence, and lasting presence. This transformation would profoundly shape its psychological and social impact, setting the stage for both resilience and conflict in the centuries to come.

Faith And Power In The Early Centuries

As Christianity became more organized and visible, it also became more threatening to existing systems of power. What had once been a quiet movement rooted in shared belief now stood as an alternative way of understanding authority, loyalty, and meaning. This shift placed early Christians in tension with religious, cultural, and political structures that already governed social life.

Power shapes how belief is received. In the early centuries, Christianity existed on the margins of society, often viewed with suspicion or hostility. Its refusal to fully conform to established religious practices and political loyalties marked it as different. This difference carried psychological weight, shaping how believers understood themselves in relation to the wider world.

Opposition did not only come from outside political forces. Early Christians also faced resistance from religious authorities who viewed the movement as a challenge to tradition and social order. These tensions created an environment where faith was practiced under pressure, reinforcing an intense sense of group identity rooted in resilience and shared struggle.

Living under threat affected the inner life of believers. Fear, courage, loyalty, and sacrifice became central emotional experiences. Faith was no longer simply a source of meaning; it became a test of commitment. For many, belief was strengthened by opposition, as shared suffering deepened bonds and reinforced a sense of purpose. At the same time, power dynamics shaped how authority developed within the Church itself. External pressure encouraged internal unity and discipline. Obedience to leaders and shared teachings became a means of preserving cohesion in the face of danger. Psychologically, this fostered trust and loyalty, but it also laid the groundwork for strong internal authority.

Persecution, whether widespread or localized, forced early Christians to confront questions of identity and allegiance. Who were they willing to obey? What beliefs were worth risking safety, status, or life itself? These questions were not abstract; they shaped daily choices and emotional life, deepening the psychological significance of faith.

Power also influenced how Christianity defined itself against the surrounding world. Boundaries between believers and non-believers became more pronounced. These boundaries strengthened internal solidarity, but they also heightened separation and mistrust. Faith became a marker of identity that carried both pride and vulnerability.

Psychologically, existing at the margins can produce both strength and strain. On one hand, shared opposition fostered courage, endurance, and a sense of moral clarity. On the other hand, constant pressure created anxiety, fear, and emotional exhaustion. Early Christian life was shaped by this tension between hope and hardship.

As Christianity navigated these power struggles, its understanding of authority evolved. Suffering became meaningful, obedience became virtuous, and endurance became a sign of faithfulness. These ideas would leave a lasting imprint on Christian thought, shaping how later generations understood sacrifice, loyalty, and moral responsibility.

Faith in the early centuries was therefore shaped not only by belief, but by power. The interaction between Christianity and external authority forged a psychological identity marked by resilience, boundary-making, and deep commitment. These experiences would continue to influence the Church as it moved into periods of greater acceptance, authority, and institutional strength, changes that would bring new challenges of their own.

Time And Periods Of The Church

1. Christianity and the Early Middle Ages (590–1048)

As the ancient world gave way to the early Middle Ages or the Medieval Age, societies across Europe faced profound instability. Political structures weakened, social order fragmented, and communities struggled to find continuity amid uncertainty. In this shifting landscape, Christianity moved from the margins toward the center of social life, offering a sense of structure, meaning, and stability when many other institutions faltered.

During this period, the Church increasingly became a source of order. It provided continuity in a time shaped by disruption, preserving knowledge, tradition, and moral guidance. For many people, faith offered reassurance in an unpredictable world. Psychologically, Christianity came to be associated with security, authority, and continuity, qualities deeply valued during times of social upheaval. Christian leaders began to play a more visible role in guiding communities. The Church emerged as a moral authority that shaped behavior, resolved disputes, and offered direction. This growing authority influenced how people understood responsibility and obedience, reinforcing the idea that faith was not only a personal matter but a guiding force for collective life.

As Christianity became more intricately linked to governance and social organization, its psychological influence expanded. Faith now shaped how individuals understood hierarchy, duty, and social roles. Obedience to religious authority often mirrored obedience within broader social structures, reinforcing patterns of trust and submission that shaped everyday life. Education also became closely tied to the Church during this period. Religious institutions preserved learning, literacy, and moral instruction, influencing how people understood knowledge and truth. Through teaching and tradition, Christianity shaped how individuals interpreted the world and their place within it, reinforcing shared values across generations.

The Church's growing presence in daily life meant that belief was no longer experienced primarily as resistance or survival, as it had been in earlier centuries. Instead, faith became associated with order and legitimacy. This shift brought psychological comfort for many, as religion provided a stable framework within which to live and understand the world. Yet increased authority also introduced new dynamics. As the Church's influence expanded, boundaries became more defined. Expectations about belief, behavior, and loyalty were reinforced more firmly. While this strengthened unity and cohesion, it also limited flexibility and dissent, shaping how individuals navigated conformity and difference.

Faith during the early Middle Ages became deeply embedded in social identity. To belong to society increasingly meant to belong within a Christian framework. This close connection between religion and social life shaped how people understood identity, morality, and community membership. Belief was not simply chosen; it was assumed as part of one's place in the world.

Psychologically, this integration of faith and society offered both reassurance and constraint. For many, Christianity provided meaning, order, and a sense of purpose. For others, it narrowed the space for alternative beliefs or identities, reinforcing social expectations that were difficult to challenge. The early Middle Ages marked a turning point in Christianity's development. Faith had moved from a position of vulnerability into one of authority and influence.

This transformation laid the groundwork for the expansion of power, structure, and control that would characterize the next period of history, where belief and authority would become even more closely intertwined.

2. Authority and Expansion in the Central Middle Ages (1048–1294)

As Christianity moved into the central Middle Ages, its influence expanded dramatically. The Church was no longer simply a stabilizing presence within society; it had become a central authority shaping political power, social order, and moral life. Faith and authority were now deeply intertwined, and Christianity's psychological impact grew alongside its institutional strength.

During this period, religious authority reached every aspect of daily life. The Church influenced laws, education, family structures, and moral expectations. For many people, Christianity was not just a belief system but the framework through which they understood life. Obedience to religious authority became intricately connected to obedience within society itself. This expansion brought an intense sense of unity. Shared belief provided a common identity that connected people across regions and cultures. Christianity offered a moral language that transcended local customs, reinforcing collective purpose and cohesion.

Psychologically, this shared identity fostered a sense of security and belonging, grounding individuals within a larger social order. At the same time, authority became more formalized. Leadership structures grew clearer, hierarchies became more rigid, and expectations were enforced more strongly. Faith was increasingly mediated through institutional power, shaping how people related to authority, discipline, and moral responsibility. Obedience was often framed as both a spiritual virtue and a social necessity.

As Christianity expanded its reach, it also defined its boundaries more sharply. Distinctions between orthodoxy and deviation became more pronounced, reinforcing control over belief and practice. These boundaries protected unity, but they also limited diversity of thought. Psychologically, this fostered conformity while discouraging questioning or dissent.

Power brought confidence, but it also introduced tension. The Church's growing authority sometimes blurred the line between spiritual guidance and social control. For some, faith provided clarity and order. For others, it became associated with fear of judgment, punishment, or exclusion. These mixed experiences shaped how belief was internalized across different social positions. The central Middle Ages also saw Christianity extend beyond spiritual leadership into cultural dominance. Religious values shaped art, education, and public life, influencing how people imagined the world and their place within it. Faith became a lens through which reality was interpreted, reinforcing both meaning and hierarchy.

Psychologically, living within a strongly religious social order influenced self-perception. Identity became closely tied to conformity with religious expectations. Moral worth was often measured through visible obedience and adherence to accepted norms. This created clear pathways to belonging, but it also intensified pressure to conform.

Despite these tensions, many found stability in the order Christianity provided. The faith offered structure in an uncertain world, guiding behavior and reinforcing social roles. For communities, this stability helped maintain cohesion. For individuals, it often brought reassurance and a sense of purpose. The central Middle Ages represent a peak in Christianity's institutional power. Faith had become deeply embedded in the structures of society, shaping both outer life and inner experience. This concentration of authority set the stage for future conflict, reform, and questioning, developments that would challenge the balance between belief, power, and human experience in the centuries that followed.

3. Crisis, Reform, and the Late Middle Ages (1305-1500)

As Christianity moved into the later Middle Ages, the unity and certainty that once defined its authority began to show signs of strain. This era is between the 14th to the 16th centuries. The structures that had provided order and stability were increasingly questioned, and confidence in religious leadership weakened.

What had once felt unshakable now appeared fragile, creating a period marked by uncertainty, tension, and psychological unease. For many believers, this era was unsettling. Faith had long been associated with clarity and moral direction, but contradictions between religious ideals and institutional practices became difficult to ignore. Corruption, internal conflict, and struggles for power challenged trust in authority.

Psychologically, this created confusion, disappointment, and a growing sense of distance between belief and lived experience. As trust weakened, calls for reform grew louder. People began to question whether the Church still reflected the values it taught. These questions were not only theological; they were deeply personal. Individuals struggled to reconcile their faith with the behavior of those in positions of authority. This tension reshaped how people related to belief, obedience, and responsibility.

The psychological impact of this crisis was profound. Where faith had once offered reassurance, it now produced doubt for some and defensiveness for others. Anxiety replaced certainty, and loyalty was assessed by frustration and disillusionment. Belief became more complex, less automatic, and more internally contested. At the same time, reform movements reflected a desire to recover meaning and authenticity. Many sought a faith that aligned more closely with moral integrity and lived experience. These efforts revealed a deep psychological need for coherence between belief, authority, and personal conscience. Faith was no longer only inherited; it was increasingly examined.

This period also intensified boundaries within Christian communities. Disagreement over belief and practice created divisions, shaping new identities and loyalties. Belonging became more conditional, and conflict replaced consensus. Psychologically, this fragmentation disrupted the sense of unity that had long characterized Christian social life. For ordinary people, navigating these changes was emotionally demanding. Long-held assumptions about authority, salvation, and moral guidance were challenged. Some responded with renewed devotion, while others withdrew or questioned more deeply. The emotional landscape of faith became more complex, marked by struggle as well as hope.

The late Middle Ages also highlighted the limits of institutional control. As challenges grew, it became clear that authority alone could not guarantee belief or loyalty. Inner conviction and conscience began to matter more, shifting the psychological center of faith from external obedience to internal reflection.

This era marked a turning point. Christianity was no longer experienced as a single, unified force but as a contested and evolving tradition. The psychological relationship between believers and authority changed, creating space for new interpretations, movements, and identities. Crisis and reform did not signal the end of Christianity's influence, but its transformation. Out of uncertainty, new ways of understanding faith, authority, and responsibility emerged. These changes set the stage for the modern period, where belief would continue to shape society, but in increasingly diverse and personal ways.

4. The Rise of the Modern Church (1517AD)

As Christianity entered the modern era, it found itself in a world shaped by rapid social change. Political structures evolved, scientific knowledge expanded, and cultural values began to shift. Faith no longer existed within a single dominant framework, but alongside new ways of understanding truth, authority, and human experience. Christianity was challenged to adapt, redefine itself, and respond to a changing society.

In this new context, religious authority became less centralized. While institutions remained influential, individuals increasingly encountered faith as a personal choice rather than an unquestioned social inheritance. This shift altered the psychological relationship between belief and belonging. Faith became something to be examined, interpreted, and, for some, reimagined. The modern Church continued to shape social life, but its influence operated in diverse ways. Christianity remained present in education, moral discourse, and community life, yet it now shared space with competing perspectives. This plurality changed how belief functioned psychologically, introducing choice, comparison, and internal negotiation into religious experience.

For many, this period brought a sense of freedom. Individuals could engage faith more personally, forming beliefs that aligned with conscience and experience. This shift encouraged reflection and self-examination, allowing belief to become more intentional rather than simply inherited. Psychologically, faith moved closer to the individual's inner life.

At the same time, this freedom introduced new challenges. Without a single authoritative framework, belief could feel uncertain or fragmented. Some experienced confusion or loss as traditional structures weakened. The security once provided by shared assumptions gave way to a need for personal meaning-making and responsibility.

The modern Church also became increasingly engaged with social issues. Christianity played a visible role in movements related to education, charity, and moral reform. Faith motivated action beyond religious spaces, influencing debates about justice, responsibility, and human dignity. Belief continued to shape behavior, even as its forms evolved.

Institutionally, churches adapted by redefining their roles within society. Emphasis shifted toward community engagement, teaching, and personal spiritual development. Rather than relying solely on authority, the modern Church often appealed to conscience, persuasion, and shared values to maintain relevance.

Psychologically, belief in the modern era became more diverse. Experiences of faith varied widely across cultures, traditions, and personal histories. Christianity can be a source of empowerment and meaning for some, while others may experience distance or tension. This diversity reflected broader changes in how people related to institutions and authority.

Despite these changes, Christianity remained a powerful influence. Its narratives, moral frameworks, and communal practices continued to shape identity and social life. Even when belief was questioned or reinterpreted, its psychological presence endured within culture and personal experience. The rise of the modern Church represents adaptation rather than decline. Christianity adjusted to new realities, continuing to shape meaning, behavior, and identity in evolving ways.

This period set the foundation for understanding how faith functions in contemporary society, where belief, choice, and social influence intersect in complex and ongoing ways.

5. Institutions, Norms, and Everyday Life (20th Century- Present)

As Christianity became woven into the fabric of society, its influence extended far beyond formal worship or religious belief. Faith began to shape the routines, expectations, and rhythms of everyday life. Through institutions such as churches, schools, and families, Christianity quietly influenced how people lived, learned, and related to one another.

Institutions play a powerful role in shaping behavior. They transmit values, reinforce norms, and define what is considered appropriate or meaningful. Christian institutions became carriers of moral instruction, teaching individuals how to behave, what to value, and how to understand responsibility. These lessons were learned not only through words, but through repetition and daily practice.

Education became one of the most significant channels of influence. Schools and learning centers shaped by Christian values helped form moral reasoning and social behavior. Through instruction and discipline, individuals absorbed ideas about authority, obedience, and purpose. Over time, these ideas became internalized, shaping character and decision-making.

Family life was also deeply influenced by Christian norms. Expectations surrounding marriage, parenting, gender roles, and responsibility were shaped by religious teaching. These norms influenced how individuals understood love, duty, and commitment. Faith entered the most intimate spaces of life, shaping relationships and personal identity.

Social norms reinforced these expectations. Community approval and disapproval communicated what was valued and what was discouraged. Christianity's moral frameworks helped regulate behavior through shared understanding rather than constant enforcement. Psychologically, this created a sense of order, guiding individuals toward accepted patterns of living.

At the same time, norms can both limit and guide. When expectations become rigid, individuals may feel constrained or judged.

Those who struggled to conform to established norms often experienced tension between personal experience and social expectation. This tension shaped emotional life, influencing self-esteem, belonging, and identity.

Institutions also reinforced authority. Religious leaders, educators, and family figures became symbols of moral guidance. Trust in these figures shaped how individuals related to power and responsibility. For many, authority offered security and clarity; for others, it became a source of fear or resentment. Daily life within faith-shaped institutions often involved routine. Rituals, schedules, and practices structured time and behavior. These routines reinforced belief through habit, embedding faith within ordinary experience. Over time, belief became part of how life was lived, even when it was not consciously reflected upon.

Psychologically, this integration of faith into everyday life created continuity. Belief was reinforced through familiarity and repetition, offering stability across generations. Yet it also reduced space for questioning, as norms became taken for granted rather than examined.

By shaping institutions, norms, and daily routines, Christianity extended its influence into the ordinary moments of life. Faith was no longer encountered only in moments of reflection or crisis, but in the everyday patterns that shaped identity, behavior, and social belonging. This deep integration prepared the ground for examining how authority, obedience, and psychological influence operate within institutional faith, an exploration that continues in the next section.

Authority, Obedience, And Psychological Influence

Authority plays a significant role in shaping how belief is lived and understood. As Christianity became institutionalized, religious authority influenced not only what people believed but also how they behaved and related to one another. Authority offered guidance and structure, helping individuals navigate moral life within an ordered social framework.

For many, obedience to religious authority provided clarity and reassurance. Clear expectations reduced uncertainty, offering a sense of direction in both personal and social life. Trust in religious leaders and institutions helped individuals feel secure, especially in complex or changing environments. Psychologically, obedience often brought comfort and stability.

Authority also shaped conscience. Teachings about right and wrong became internalized, guiding behavior even in the absence of direct supervision. Over time, external rules became internal standards, shaping thought patterns, emotional responses, and self-evaluation. This internalization demonstrates how deeply institutional influence can reach into the human mind. Yet obedience is rarely experienced in only one way. While some found security in authority, others experienced pressure or fear. When authority was perceived as rigid or punitive, belief could become associated with anxiety or guilt. The psychological impact of authority depended on how it was exercised and interpreted.

Power dynamics within religious institutions also shaped social relationships. Hierarchies influenced who had voice, influence, and legitimacy. These dynamics affected how individuals understood worth, responsibility, and belonging. Authority could elevate, but it could also marginalize, shaping psychological experience in lasting ways. Obedience was often framed as moral virtue. Faithfulness was associated with submission to established norms and leaders. This framing reinforced conformity and strengthened institutional cohesion. Psychologically, it encouraged self-discipline and restraint, but it also limited space for questioning or dissent.

At times, authority and obedience became tools of control. When belief was enforced without compassion or reflection, it risked suppressing individuality and conscience. Individuals who struggled to conform often faced inner conflict, balancing their personal experience with institutional expectations.

Despite these challenges, authority also enabled continuity. It preserved belief across generations, maintained shared identity, and sustained community life. Many individuals experienced authority not as coercion, but as guidance that supported moral growth and social responsibility.

The psychological influence of authority lies in its ability to shape both behavior and inner life. Obedience becomes meaningful when it aligns with personal values and shared purpose. When misaligned, it can produce tension and resistance. Understanding this balance is essential to understanding faith's impact on society.

As Christianity moved through history, authority and obedience remained central to its influence. These dynamics continue to shape how belief is experienced today, informing debates about power, responsibility, and belonging. With this understanding, we are prepared to reflect on how historical development connects to ongoing social and psychological consequences, a reflection that leads us into the next chapter.

From History To Social Impact

The historical development of Christianity reveals more than a sequence of events; it reveals how belief becomes embedded in human life. From a small movement rooted in shared experience to a powerful institution shaping societies, Christianity's journey illustrates how faith evolves alongside social structures, authority, and culture. History shows us not only what Christianity became, but how its influence took shape over time.

Across each stage of development, belief interacted with human needs for meaning, belonging, and order. Early communities relied on shared identity and resilience. Institutional growth introduced structure and authority. Periods of crisis exposed tension between belief and power. Each phase shaped how faith was experienced psychologically, how people understood themselves, how they related to authority, and how they found purpose within society.

As Christianity gained influence, its impact

extended beyond religious spaces into social systems that governed daily life. Laws, education, family structures, and moral norms reflected religious values shaped over centuries of institutional development. These influences did not remain abstract; they shaped real experiences, expectations, and behaviors across generations.

The psychological consequences of this development are complex. For some, Christianity provided stability, moral clarity, and a sense of belonging. For others, it introduced pressure, fear, or exclusion. These differing experiences reflect how belief, once institutionalized, affects people differently depending on their position within social structures and power relationships.

History also reveals that faith and authority are never neutral. As Christianity became intertwined with political and cultural power, it shaped social boundaries, defining who belonged, who was trusted, and who was excluded. These boundaries carried psychological weight, influencing identity, self-worth, and social standing. Understanding this historical foundation helps explain why Christianity continues to shape social life today. The patterns established over centuries, authority, obedience, moral expectations, and institutional influence, did not disappear over time. They continue to inform how belief is experienced, challenged, and negotiated in contemporary society.

This chapter has shown that Christianity's psychological impact cannot be separated from its historical development. Belief does not float above society; it is carried through institutions, traditions, and power structures that shape human experience. History provides the context needed to understand why faith affects people as it does. With this historical lens in place, we are now prepared to examine the lived consequences of Christianity's social influence. The next chapter turns toward moments of conflict and exclusion, exploring how discrimination, persecution, and social boundaries shaped early Christian identity and psychological experience.

What follows is not a departure from history, but a deeper engagement with its effects. Chapter Three moves from institutional development to human experience, examining how faith, identity, and power intersected in moments of tension, shaping both collective behavior and the inner lives of those who lived within and beyond Christianity's boundaries.

Reflective Pause

✓ History leaves traces in the present. The journey of Christianity from movement to institution shaped not only belief, but authority, social order, and psychological life. Across centuries, faith became embedded in structures that guided behavior, defined belonging, and influenced identity.

✓ Some experienced this development as stability and guidance; others encountered it as pressure or exclusion. These differing experiences reveal how power, authority, and belief intersect in human life. History reminds us that faith is never lived in isolation; it is carried through systems that shape both opportunity and limitation.

✓   As you pause, consider how historical structures continue to influence belief today. Reflect on how authority, tradition, and institutional expectations shape personal experience and social life. Understanding the past helps illuminate the present and prepares us to engage more thoughtfully with the challenges that follow.

The Bridge

History shows how belief becomes embedded in power, structure, and social life. As Christianity grew from a movement into an institution, it shaped authority, identity, and moral order in ways that reached far beyond individual belief. These developments brought stability to some, but also produced tension, conflict, and exclusion for others.

The structures and boundaries formed over time not only defined what Christianity stood for; they also defined who belonged and who did not. As authority solidified, differences in belief, culture, and identity increasingly became points of division. Faith, once centered on shared community, became entangled with questions of loyalty, conformity, and power.

Chapter Three turns toward these moments of tension. It examines how discrimination, persecution, and social conflict shaped early Christian identity and psychological experience. Moving from institutional development to living struggle, the next chapter explores how faith was experienced under pressure, and how conflict left lasting marks on both belief and the human mind.

CHAPTER THREE

DISCRIMINATION IN THE EARLY CENTURIES AND ITS PSYCHOLOGICAL IMPLICATIONS

C hristianity did not develop in a social vacuum. From its earliest days, it appeared within environments marked by tension, suspicion, and resistance. As the faith took shape, it encountered opposition from religious authorities, cultural traditions, and political powers. These encounters were not merely historical events; they were deeply human experiences that shaped how belief was lived, understood, and internalized.

Discrimination and exclusion played a formative role in early Christian life. Paraphrasing Webmaster's idea on discrimination, it is not a new phenomenon; rather, it is an integral part of human history. (Webmaster, 2025) Though in today's scenario we understand discrimination as an unfair or prejudicial treatment of different sections of society, particularly on the basis of race, age, gender, or any other disability, its history goes back to the beginning of humankind. To believe was often to stand apart, to risk rejection, and to navigate uncertainty. These pressures shaped identity, strengthened group bonds, and influenced how early believers understood loyalty, sacrifice, and belonging.

Faith was not only professed but also evaluated under social and psychological strain.

This chapter explores how discrimination shaped early Christianity from within. It examines moments of rejection, conflict, and persecution not simply as external challenges but as forces that shape emotional life, group behavior, and identity formation. Living under pressure shaped how believers understood themselves and others, reinforcing boundaries and deepening commitment while also creating fear and division.

Discrimination did not come from a sole source. Early Christians faced opposition from religious authorities who questioned their legitimacy, from cultural systems that resisted change, and from political powers that viewed the movement as a threat to order. These layers of conflict created complex psychological experiences, resilience, and courage on one hand, anxiety, and vulnerability on the other.

At the same time, conflict appeared within the Christian community itself. Questions about belonging, authority, and belief created internal divisions that were often just as psychologically demanding as external persecution. The struggle to define identity and preserve unity introduced new forms of exclusion and control that would leave lasting marks on Christian social life. This chapter does not approach these realities to condemn or defend, but to understand. By examining discrimination and conflict through a psychological lens, we gain insight into how belief is shaped under pressure and how identity forms in response to exclusion. These early experiences help explain later patterns of authority, boundary-making, and social influence.

As we move through this chapter, the focus is still on human experience, on fear, courage, belonging, and struggle. Understanding these dynamics allows us to see how faith shaped not only doctrine and practice, but also emotional life and social behavior. The experiences explored here form a critical link between Christianity's historical development and its later social impact. Out of the struggle, resilience appeared, but also rigid boundaries. Out of persecution grew both unity and systems of control. These tensions continue to echo through history, shaping how belief interacts with society today.

Brief History Of Discrimination From The Early Centuries

Historically, discrimination was based on instincts such as survival, tribalism, and protection of resources, and this led early human beings to adopt a very hierarchical structure in their societies, considering kinship, class, and purity while discriminating against others. **Ancient Egyptian, Greek, and Roman** civilizations have a history of institutionalized discrimination against minority groups such as slaves and foreigners. Women have also been discriminated against and have been considered inferior to men in legal and social contexts, and early Christians in the Roman Empire have also been discriminated against for their religious beliefs and practices. Laws in Mesopotamia, India, and China have institutionalized such discriminative practices and have laid down severe punishments for such acts (Webmaster 2025).

From the religious perspective, with the development of empires, new systems of discrimination arose, which were, in turn, affected by religious teachings and cultural nationalism. The Middle Ages were characterized by religious affiliation as a significant source of discrimination, especially for Jewish populations in a Christian-dominated Europe, who were subjected to exclusion, persecution, and discriminatory legislation. Taking into account, the period of European colonialism further solidified systems of discrimination, especially through the transatlantic slave trade, where millions of Africans were forcibly made slaves through racial hierarchies that labeled them as less than human. Colonial regimes-maintained separation between racial and ethnic groups, favoring European colonizers over Indigenous groups and workers, with these differences being codified into law to deny fundamental rights to the colonized.

While the history of discrimination has been long, difficult, and complex, it has also been a story that has not been written in stone. Every generation has been an opportunity to address injustice, destroy antiquated thinking, and build a society upon justice and dignity. To support this claim, Gaines and Reed argues that "racism is not a universal feature of human psychology but a historically developed process. Racism begins with the exploitation of people or peoples and with the psychological consequences to which that exploitation leads" (Gaines and Reed 1995, 96-103).

History has shown us how prejudice has been a tool for domination and separation, but it has also been a reminder that activism, opposition, and law can be a powerful force for change. Knowing how we have been can help us know how we are going, and how we can preserve our freedoms and liberties for future generations.

Identity Under Pressure

Identity is often shaped most powerfully under pressure. When people are accepted, belonging feels natural and unexamined. When they are rejected or marginalized, identity becomes something that must be defended, protected, and clarified. For early Christians, belief was not merely a private conviction; it was a public marker that often placed them at odds with their surrounding societies.

Living as a minority shaped how early believers understood themselves. Their faith set them apart socially, culturally, and, at times, legally. This sense of difference fostered a strong internal identity, defined by shared beliefs, mutual support, and collective resilience. Psychological strength emerged from shared vulnerability.

Pressure reinforced group cohesion. Facing opposition together deepened loyalty and trust within the community. Belonging took on heightened importance, as relationships within the group provided safety and affirmation when acceptance elsewhere was limited. Identity became closely tied to community membership, strengthening emotional bonds. At the same time, living under constant scrutiny produced psychological strain. Fear of rejection, punishment, or loss affected emotional life. Believers had to navigate daily decisions with awareness of social consequences. Faith became something to be protected, sometimes hidden, sometimes boldly affirmed, depending on circumstance.

Identity under pressure often becomes simplified. Clear distinctions appear between "us" and "them," reinforcing group boundaries. These distinctions helped early Christians preserve their beliefs, but they also narrowed their perspective. Psychological clarity was gained through contrast, even as complexity was reduced.

Belief under threat encouraged commitment. Choosing faith carried weight, and this seriousness strengthened identity. Faithfulness became a marker of courage and loyalty. Endurance under hardship was not only admired; it became central to how believers understood what it meant to belong. However, pressure also shaped conformity. When survival depends on unity, deviation can feel dangerous. Early communities often emphasized shared belief and behavior to preserve cohesion.

Psychologically, this fostered loyalty but also discouraged questioning or differences within the group. For some, pressure intensified personal conviction. Faith offered meaning, helping interpret suffering as purposeful rather than random. This reframing supported emotional resilience, allowing individuals to endure hardship with a sense of direction and hope.

For others, pressure produced inner conflict. Fear, doubt, and exhaustion went with the effort to remain faithful under threat. Identity was not always experienced as a source of strength; at times, it became a burden, laden with expectations and risks. Identity under pressure shaped the future of Christianity. The patterns formed in these early moments have strong group bonds, clear boundaries, and deep commitment, which would continue to influence how the faith understood belonging, loyalty, and difference. These psychological foundations set the stage for later conflicts and divisions explored in the sections that follow.

Religious Discrimination And Internal Conflict

The earliest conflicts faced by Christians did not arise solely from distant political powers; many also came from within familiar religious spaces. Christianity appeared from within Judaism, sharing sacred texts, traditions, and moral foundations. This closeness made separation especially painful. What felt to some like faithful continuity felt to others like a dangerous departure.

Religious authorities viewed the new movement with suspicion. Belief in Jesus as Messiah challenged established interpretations, leadership, and religious order. For early Christians, rejection by familiar religious communities carried a deep psychological weight. Being excluded from a tradition that once felt like home intensified feelings of loss, confusion, and vulnerability.

Discrimination rooted in religious disagreement often strikes at identity. Faith is rarely just belief; it is heritage, memory, and belonging. When early Christians were rejected or marginalized by Jewish authorities, they were not only dismissed intellectually, but they were also separated emotionally and socially. This separation reshaped how they understood themselves and their place in the religious world.

This rejection also forced early believers to clarify who they were becoming. Boundaries that once felt shared now required definition. Identity had to be reconstructed in response to exclusion. Psychologically, this process involved grief for what was lost and a resolve to protect what remained.

Conflict with religious authority strengthened internal cohesion, but it also hardened divisions. Early Christian communities emphasized shared belief and loyalty as protection against rejection. Unity became essential for survival, reinforcing group identity while reducing openness to difference. Belief became more clearly defined in contrast to what it was not. At the same time, internal conflict appeared. Questions about tradition, authority, and interpretation created tension within Christian communities themselves. Disagreement was not merely intellectual; it carried emotional consequences. Fear of rejection, accusation, or exclusion shaped how people expressed belief and navigated disagreement.

Psychologically, living within a contested religious space demanded constant negotiation. Believers balanced reverence for inherited tradition with commitment to new conviction. This tension shaped emotional life, producing courage for some and anxiety for others. Faith was not only affirmed but also evaluated by loss and uncertainty.

Discrimination also shaped the development of

authority within Christianity. Rejection from outside groups encouraged internal consolidation. Leaders gained influence as protectors of belief and identity. While this offered security, it also laid the groundwork for rigid boundaries and heightened control over belief. For many, suffering religious rejection deepened commitment. Faith became meaningful precisely because it required sacrifice.

Endurance under exclusion strengthened resolve and reinforced the idea that belief was worth personal cost. This framing transformed pain into purpose. Religious discrimination in the early centuries, therefore, shaped Christianity in lasting ways. It forged identity through separation, strengthened internal bonds, and introduced patterns of boundary-making that would reappear throughout history. These experiences remind us that beliefs formed under pressure often carry both resilience and rigidity, forces that continue to shape religious life today.

Race, Difference, And Early Social Division

As Christianity spread beyond its original cultural setting, questions of difference became unavoidable. What began within a shared religious and cultural world now met diverse languages, ethnic identities, and social customs. These differences shaped how belief was received, practiced, and understood, introducing new layers of complexity into early Christian life. Han S. 2018 wrote...

Racial discrimination in social behavior, although disapproved of by many contemporary cultures, has been widely reported. Because empathy plays a key functional role in social behavior, brain imaging researchers have extensively investigated the neurocognitive underpinnings of racial ingroup bias in empathy. This research has revealed consistent evidence for increased neural responses to the perceived pain of same-race compared with other-race individuals in multiple brain regions and across multiple time-windows. Although ingroup bias in empathic brain activity has been widely documented, both laboratory manipulations and real-life interracial experiences can reduce racial ingroup bias in empathy by increasing empathic neural responses to other-race pain (Han 2018, 420).

The truth is that his findings have crucial implications for understanding racial ingroup preference in social behavior, as well as increasing interracial communication. Because differences often bring opportunity but also tension. Early Christian communities struggled to navigate cultural diversity while preserving shared belief. Ethnic and racial distinctions, though not defined in modern terms, shaped how individuals were perceived, valued, and included. Belonging was influenced not only by belief, but by culture and background.

For many early believers, entering the Christian community required navigating unfamiliar social expectations. Language, customs, and social norms varied across regions, influencing how faith was expressed and understood.

These differences could enrich community life, but they also exposed underlying hierarchies and biases that shaped inclusion. Psychologically, difference affects identity. When individuals perceive themselves as culturally or ethnically distinct, they may experience uncertainty about belonging. Early Christians from marginalized backgrounds often had to negotiate their place within communities shaped by dominant cultural norms. This negotiation shaped emotional life, influencing confidence, vulnerability, and self-worth.

Social division often appears when differences are perceived as a threat. As Christianity expanded, some communities responded to diversity with openness, while others responded with caution or exclusion. These responses reflected deeper fears about losing identity, authority, or tradition. Difference became something to manage rather than embrace. Within these dynamics, power played a significant role. Cultural dominance influenced which practices were considered normative and which were viewed as secondary. Those aligned with dominant cultural expressions of faith often enjoyed greater acceptance, while others were expected to adapt. Psychologically, this created pressure to conform and suppress differences.

Racial and cultural distinctions also shaped leadership and voice. Certain groups held greater influence in shaping beliefs and practices, thereby reinforcing social hierarchies within the faith community. These hierarchies affected how individuals understood legitimacy and belonging, shaping long-term patterns of inclusion and exclusion. For those pushed to the margins, faith became a complex experience. Christianity offered spiritual belonging while simultaneously reflecting social inequality. This tension produced inner conflict, as individuals sought affirmation within a system that did not always fully recognize their identity or experience.

Yet differences also fostered resilience. Marginalized believers often developed strong internal identity and spiritual resolve. Faith became a source of dignity and hope, offering meaning that transcended social position.

These psychological resources helped individuals endure exclusion while staying committed to their beliefs. At the communal level, social division challenged unity.

Communities struggled to reconcile the message of inclusion with practices shaped by cultural bias. This contradiction introduced tension that shaped how belief was interpreted and lived. Faith communities became sites of both connection and conflict. These early experiences of difference left lasting impressions. Patterns of cultural dominance and marginalization established during this period would reappear throughout Christian history. The psychological effects of pressure conform, fear of exclusion, and internalized hierarchy continued to shape the relationship between faith and identity.

Race and difference in early Christianity remind us that belief is always lived within social structures. Faith does not erase difference automatically; it encounters it. How communities respond to difference shapes not only social relationships but also the inner lives of those who seek belonging within them.

The Crisis Of Circumcision And Gentile Inclusion

As Christianity continued to spread, one question became unavoidable: *Who truly belonged?* The growing presence of Gentile believers forced early Christian communities to confront long-held assumptions about identity, tradition, and inclusion. What had once been a faith rooted in a specific cultural and religious context now faced the challenge of expansion beyond those boundaries.

Circumcision was not merely a physical practice; it was a powerful symbol of identity, covenant, and belonging. For Jewish believers, it represented continuity with tradition and faithfulness to inherited religious life. For Gentile converts, the requirement felt foreign and burdensome. The question of circumcision, therefore, became a deeper question about access, legitimacy, and acceptance. Psychologically, this debate carried significant weight. Belonging is not only about belief; it is about recognition. Gentile believers faced uncertainty about whether their faith was sufficient or conditional. The pressure to conform to unfamiliar practices introduced anxiety, self-doubt, and fear of exclusion.

For Jewish Christians, the situation also produced tension. Tradition provided stability and meaning, and the fear of losing cultural identity felt real. The inclusion of Gentiles raised concerns about diluting faith and losing distinctiveness. These fears reflected a common psychological response to change, protecting identity when boundaries feel threatened. The debate forced communities to confront the difference between faith as conviction and faith as cultural inheritance. Should belonging be defined by belief alone, or by adherence to established practices? This question reshaped how early Christians understood identity, commitment, and spiritual legitimacy.

Community discussions around circumcision revealed the emotional cost of boundary-making. Decisions about inclusion affected real lives, shaping who felt welcomed and who felt burdened. These debates were not abstract theological arguments; they were lived experiences that shaped confidence, belonging, and emotional well-being. For Gentile believers, conditional acceptance created internal conflict. Faith offered spiritual belonging, yet social belonging felt uncertain. This tension produced a psychological strain familiar to many marginalized groups, the sense of being included in principle but excluded in practice.

At the same time, resistance to circumcision became an act of self-definition. Gentile believers asserted that faith should not require cultural erasure. This assertion strengthened a sense of identity rooted in belief rather than tradition, reinforcing the idea that belonging could be spiritual rather than ethnic.

The resolution of this crisis reshaped Christianity's future. By redefining the basis of belonging, early communities moved toward a more inclusive identity. Psychologically, this shift allowed faith to be experienced as accessible rather than conditional, reducing barriers to participation and belonging. Yet the process left lasting marks. The struggle over inclusion revealed how deeply fear, power, and identity influence religious life. Even when inclusion was affirmed, the memory of exclusion lingered, shaping how communities understood authority and difference.

This crisis also set a pattern: debates about

belonging often emerge during periods of growth. Expansion forces communities to choose between protection and openness.

The psychological tension between preserving identity and embracing diversity would reappear throughout Christian history. The crisis of circumcision and Gentile inclusion shows that inclusion is rarely simple. It requires confronting fear, relinquishing control, and redefining identity. These early struggles shaped Christianity's understanding of belonging and set precedents for how faith would respond to difference in subsequent generations.

Persecution By Roman Authority

As Christianity continued to grow, it drew the attention of Roman authority. What had once been a small and fragmented movement became increasingly visible, and visibility brought risk. Roman power was built on loyalty, order, and public conformity, and Christianity's refusal to fully align with these expectations marked it as a threat to social stability.

For early Christians, persecution was not merely an abstract concept; it was a lived reality. Arrest, punishment, and social exclusion created an atmosphere of fear and uncertainty. Believers learned to live with the awareness that faith could carry profound consequences. This constant threat shaped emotional life, influencing decisions, relationships, and daily behavior.

Psychologically, persecution intensified identity. When belief carries cost, it becomes more deeply internalized. Choosing faith in the face of threat transformed belief into commitment. Loyalty to faith was no longer symbolic; it was evaluated through endurance and sacrifice. This pressure strengthened group bonds and reinforced a shared sense of purpose.

Fear played a vital role in this experience. Fear of punishment, loss, or death affected how believers expressed faith publicly and privately. Some practiced caution, while others responded with defiance. These different responses reflected varying psychological coping strategies in response to threat.

Persecution also reshaped how suffering was understood. Hardship was no longer seen merely as misfortune, but as meaningful struggle.

Faith offered a framework that interpreted suffering as purposeful, transforming pain into testimony and endurance into virtue. This reframing supported emotional resilience and helped believers endure fear with hope.

At the same time, persecution created trauma. Living under constant threat strained emotional well-being. Anxiety, grief, and exhaustion accompanied the effort to remain faithful. While narratives of courage and endurance are often emphasized, the psychological toll of persecution was real and lasting. Group solidarity became a critical source of support. Community provided safety, affirmation, and shared strength. Relationships within the faith community mitigated fear and isolation, reinforcing a sense of belonging amid hostility from the wider society. Psychological survival depended heavily on collective support.

Persecution also sharpened boundaries. Loyalty was evaluated, and trust became selective. Communities grew cautious, sometimes suspicious, as fear of betrayal increased. These dynamics shaped how authority and discipline were exercised within the group, reinforcing conformity as a means of protection. The experience of persecution shaped perceptions of authority. Leaders who guided communities through danger gained trust and influence. Obedience to leadership became associated with survival and faithfulness, shaping long-term attitudes toward authority and discipline within Christianity.

For some, persecution strengthened faith; for others, it created doubt or withdrawal. Not all endured in the same way. These varied responses highlight the complexity of belief under pressure and remind us that resilience is not uniform. Faith interacts differently with individual emotional capacity and circumstance.

Roman persecution left a deep imprint on Christian psychology. It shaped narratives of sacrifice, courage, and endurance that would be carried forward into later generations. These stories became central to Christianity's understanding of faithfulness and identity.

Persecution by Roman authority reveals how power shapes belief from the outside. It forged resilience, deepened commitment, and strengthened community, but it also introduced fear, trauma, and rigid boundaries. These experiences would continue to influence how Christianity understood suffering, loyalty, and authority long after persecution itself subsided.

The Crisis Of Heresy And Internal Policing

As external persecution gradually lessened in some regions, new challenges emerged from within the Christian community itself. The threat was no longer merely external opposition but internal disagreement over belief, authority, and interpretation. Questions about what constituted "true" faith became central, with significant psychological and social consequences.

Heresy was not simply about ideas; it was about identity and control. Defining correct belief became a means of protecting unity, preserving authority, and maintaining social order. Communities that had once bonded through shared vulnerability now faced the task of regulating belief from within, shifting the source of pressure inward.

Psychologically, internal policing created a new kind of fear. Whereas persecution by external authorities involved visible danger, accusations of heresy threatened belonging itself. To be labeled deviant was to risk exclusion, loss of identity, and separation from the community. Fear of being "wrong" replaced fear of being punished.

This fear influenced how individuals expressed their beliefs. Questioning, doubt, or alternative interpretations became risky. Many learned to silence their uncertainty, conform outwardly, or suppress internal conflict to remain accepted. Over time, this environment shaped emotional life, encouraging caution and self-monitoring. Authority grew stronger amid internal division. Leaders assumed greater responsibility for defining belief and enforcing boundaries. This consolidation of power offered clarity and stability, but it also narrowed acceptable expression. Obedience became closely tied to faithfulness, reinforcing conformity as a moral expectation.

Internal policing reshaped trust within the community. Believers became more vigilant, sometimes wary of one another. Suspicion replaced openness, and loyalty was measured through alignment with approved beliefs. These dynamics altered relationships, introducing psychological distance where intimacy had once existed. For some, clear boundaries provided reassurance. Knowing what's "right" reduced uncertainty and offered a sense of security. Structure and definition helped preserve shared identity amid disagreement. Psychologically, this clarity could feel grounding and protective.

For others, however, rigid boundaries produced strain. Individuals whose experiences or insights did not align neatly with accepted beliefs often felt isolated. The pressure to conform created inner conflict, as personal conviction clashed with communal expectation. Faith became a source of anxiety rather than comfort. The policing of belief also shaped moral judgment. Deviance was framed not merely as difference, but as danger. This framing justified exclusion and reinforced the idea that unity required control. Psychologically, this encouraged binary thinking, right versus wrong, faithful versus unfaithful, reducing space for nuance or complexity.

These patterns left lasting impressions. The impulse to define, regulate, and protect belief became embedded in Christian institutional life. While this preserved doctrinal continuity, it also normalized mechanisms of exclusion that would reappear throughout history. Internal conflict revealed that communities shaped by trauma and threat often seek safety through control. What begins as protection can evolve into suppression. Understanding this dynamic helps explain how systems formed under pressure can unintentionally reproduce fear within their own boundaries.

The crisis of heresy and internal policing marks a critical moment in Christianity's development. It shows how a faith shaped by persecution can turn inward, guarding unity through control. These early patterns of boundary-making and authority would continue to influence how Christianity responded to difference, dissent, and identity in the centuries that followed.

Reflective Pause

✓ Discrimination leaves marks that go deeper than history can record. It shapes how people see themselves, how they relate to others, and how they understand belonging. The experiences explored in this chapter reveal how belief, when lived under pressure, can strengthen identity while also hardening boundaries.

✓ For early Christians, faith was shaped through rejection, fear, courage, and resilience. These experiences forged deep commitment, but they also introduced patterns of exclusion and control that would echo far beyond their time. Struggle formed character, but it also shaped how difference was managed and how authority was exercised.

✓ As you pause, consider how exclusion and acceptance shape contemporary belief. Reflect on how pressure, whether social, cultural, or institutional, shapes identity and emotional life. The forces at work in early Christianity are not confined to the past; they continue to surface wherever belonging is conditional, and belief is evaluated.

✓ This moment of reflection is not about assigning blame or praise. It concerns recognizing the human cost of discrimination and the psychological burden of living at the margins. Understanding these experiences prepares us to see how a faith shaped by struggle could later become a force for social contribution and at times, contradiction.

The Bridge

The story of Christianity does not end with discrimination, persecution, or internal conflict. The same faith shaped by struggle also became a source of meaning, resilience, and social contribution. Experiences of exclusion and hardship not only hardened boundaries; they also forged values that would later shape communities' understandings of justice, care, and responsibility.

Out of persecution emerged compassion. Out of marginalization grew concern for the vulnerable. The psychological strength developed under pressure helped shape a moral vision that emphasized dignity, service, and community life. These values would go on to influence laws, education, family structures, and social norms across societies.

Chapter Four turns toward this other side of Christianity's impact. It explores the positive psychological and social contributions that emerged over time, how faith helped shape ideas about human worth, moral responsibility, learning, and social order. This shift does not erase the tensions explored earlier; instead, it reveals the complexity of a tradition capable of both harm and healing.

By moving from conflict to contribution, the next chapter invites a more balanced understanding. It asks how a faith forged in struggle came to influence society constructively, shaping systems and values that continue to affect lives today.

CRITICAL THOUGHT

Before We Go Further, It
Is Worth Pausing.

The journey so far has taken us through belief, identity, authority, conflict, and exclusion. We have seen how Christianity shaped both the social world and the inner life, how faith formed identity under pressure, how authority emerged in response to threat, and how boundaries were drawn in moments of fear and survival. These chapters were not meant to persuade or accuse, but to illuminate how belief is lived when it intersects with power, belonging, and vulnerability.

If some of what you have read feels unsettling, that response matters. Discomfort is often a sign that something real has been touched. This book was never meant to be read at a distance. It invites attentiveness not only to history, but to the human experience beneath it.

At this point, it may be tempting to reach conclusions. To decide whether Christianity has been more harmful or more healing, more oppressive or more redemptive. But understanding rarely grows in haste. Meaning deepens when we resist the urge to simplify. Some questions are not meant to be answered quickly.

1. What happens to belief when it is shaped more by threat than by freedom?
2. How does a faith formed under exclusion later define belonging?
3. When does unity protect, and when does it

silence?

4. How do systems created for survival become systems of control?

These questions are not here to accuse the past or judge the present, rather they are here to open space for honesty.

And Now, A Word Directly To You, The Reader.

You may be coming to this book with faith that has sustained you, or with wounds left by a belief that once promised safety. You may be reading with curiosity, skepticism, devotion, or quiet searching. Wherever you stand, you are not expected to arrive at an agreement. You are invited to remain attentive to your thoughts, your emotions, and your reactions as you read.

If you find yourself defending, resisting, grieving, or recognizing pieces of your own experience in these pages, pause there. Those moments often reveal more than certainty ever could. Faith not only shapes societies, but also shapes people. And people carry stories that do not fit neatly into categories of good or bad. Before moving on, it is important to say this clearly: you are not required to resolve anything here. You do not need to decide what you believe, defend what you hold, or abandon what has shaped you. This space is not a test. It is a place to notice.

If faith has been a source of strength, that strength is not dismissed. If belief has left scars, those scars are not minimized. Both realities can coexist without canceling each other out. Understanding does not demand certainty; it asks for honesty. This book does not seek to strip belief of meaning or wrap it in protection. It seeks to understand how belief lives in human beings, shapes minds, relationships, and societies, and changes when power and vulnerability collide.

So, take a breath here. Let the weight of what you have read settle. You are neither behind nor ahead. You are exactly where the journey intends you to be. As we move into the second half of this book, the focus will shift. The chapters that follow will examine Christianity's positive psychological and social contributions, as well as its influence on human dignity, education, moral responsibility, family life, and social care. They will also confront difficult realities: cultural suppression, gender inequality, social boundaries, and the experiences of those pushed to the margins.

What comes next requires a particular posture: not judgment but curiosity, not defense but openness, not dismissal but discernment. Before we go further, consider carrying this tension with you: a faith capable of healing can also harm; a belief born in suffering can both protect and exclude. Holding this tension is not weakness; it is maturity. Now, we go further not to arrive at easy answers, but to understand more deeply how belief continues to shape minds, communities, and lives.

CHAPTER FOUR

POSITIVE PSYCHOLOGICAL AND SOCIAL CONTRIBUTIONS

The story of Christianity is often told through moments of conflict, exclusion, and struggle. Yet that is not the whole story. Alongside tension and contradiction, Christianity has also contributed to systems of meaning, care, and social responsibility that have shaped societies in lasting ways. To understand the psychological impact of Christianity on society, it is necessary to examine not only where faith has caused harm, but also where it has fostered stability, dignity, and hope.

This chapter turns toward those contributions. It explores how Christianity has influenced moral frameworks, social relationships, and collective responsibility, offering psychological resources that helped individuals and communities navigate uncertainty, suffering, and change. These contributions did not emerge in isolation; they were shaped by history, culture, and the very struggles explored in earlier chapters. For many, Christianity provided a language of human worth and moral obligation that strengthened social bonds. Ideas about compassion, forgiveness, responsibility, and care for others influenced how communities understood justice and social order. Faith offered not only belief, but practices that encouraged belonging, cooperation, and resilience.

At the psychological level, Christianity contributed to meaning-making and emotional support. It offered frameworks for interpreting suffering, cultivating hope, and sustaining purpose across generations. In times of instability, these frameworks helped individuals endure hardship and find coherence in life's uncertainties. This chapter does not present Christianity as flawless or universally benevolent. Instead, it examines how faith functioned as a social and psychological resource, shaping laws, education, family life, and moral norms that often promote cohesion and care. These contributions exist alongside the tensions already explored, forming a fuller and more honest picture.

As we move through this chapter, the focus remains on lived experience. How did faith influence daily life? How did it shape behavior, relationships, and emotional well-being? And how did psychological needs for meaning, belonging, and order find expression through religious life? By exploring these questions, Chapter Four offers balance. It acknowledges the capacity of belief to contribute positively to society while remaining attentive to complexity. This perspective allows us to see Christianity not as a single force with a single outcome, but as a tradition whose influence has been shaped by human needs, choices, and social contexts.

What follows is an exploration of how Christianity contributed to social stability, moral development, education, and the foundations of family life, which continue to influence societies today and set the stage for the more challenging conversations that follow in later chapters.

Meaning, Belonging, And Psychological Stability

Across societies and historical periods, people have sought meaning, particularly during times of uncertainty, loss, and social change. Christianity functioned as one of the frameworks through which individuals and communities interpreted their lives and experiences. By offering explanations for suffering, purpose, and moral responsibility, faith contributed to psychological stability for many who lived within its influence.

Meaning is not only philosophical; it is psychological. When individuals can connect their experiences to a larger narrative, distress often becomes more manageable. Christianity provided narratives that helped people understand hardship not as random, but as part of a broader moral or spiritual story. This reform supported emotional endurance and reduced feelings of chaos or helplessness.

Belonging played a vital role in this process. Christian communities provided structured social spaces in which individuals could find recognition and connection. Shared beliefs, rituals, and moral expectations created a sense of collective identity, strengthening social bonds. Psychologically, belonging reduced isolation and reinforced emotional security.

For many, faith communities served as stabilizing

environments. They provided continuity across generations, preserving shared values and practices. This consistency helped individuals navigate social change with a sense of rootedness. Stability did not come from certainty alone, but from shared participation in a meaningful social world.

Christian practices reinforced this sense of order. Regular gatherings, shared rituals, and moral instruction structured daily life. These practices offered predictability and rhythm, which are known psychological supports in times of uncertainty. Through repetition and shared experience, belief became woven into everyday life. At the emotional level, Christianity offered language for hope and reassurance. Teachings that emphasized forgiveness, redemption, and renewal helped individuals cope with guilt, failure, and fear. These psychological resources supported emotional regulation and resilience, particularly in contexts marked by hardship or instability.

Faith also contributed to identity formation. Individuals often understood themselves through moral and relational roles shaped by their beliefs, such as a responsibility to others, a commitment to community, and accountability beyond the self. These identities provided direction and coherence, reinforcing a sense of purpose. Social cohesion further strengthened psychological stability. Shared moral expectations encouraged cooperation and mutual responsibility. When individuals believed they were part of a larger moral community, their behavior was guided by collective values rather than by impulse alone. This alignment between belief and behavior supported social order and personal regulation.

At the same time, meaning and belonging were not experienced uniformly. Access to community and affirmation depended on social position, conformity, and inclusion. While faith provided stability for many, it could also reinforce boundaries that limited belonging for others. These tensions remain important to acknowledge even within positive contributions. Despite these limitations, the psychological role of Christianity as a source of meaning cannot be dismissed. For centuries, faith helped individuals endure uncertainty, loss, and change by offering interpretive frameworks that support emotional life. Meaning functioned as a stabilizing force within both individual psychology and collective experience.

This stability extended beyond individuals to communities. Shared belief contributed to social continuity, helping societies maintain coherence during periods of transition. Psychological security was reinforced through collective identity, shared moral language, and mutual support. Understanding Christianity's role in meaning-making and belonging clarifies how belief functioned as a psychological resource within society. These contributions lay the foundation for examining how faith shaped moral systems, social norms, and institutional life, topics explored in the sections that follow.

Moral Frameworks, Laws, And Social Norms

Moral frameworks play a vital role in shaping how societies function. They influence behavior, define responsibility, and guide social interaction. Christianity contributed to the development of shared moral understandings that helped regulate conduct within communities. These frameworks did not operate only at the level of belief; they shaped expectations about how people ought to live together.

From a social psychological perspective, moral norms help create predictability. When individuals share an understanding of acceptable behavior, social interaction becomes more stable. Christianity offered moral guidelines that reinforced ideas of accountability, restraint, and responsibility to others. These shared expectations supported cooperation and social order. Christian moral teaching emphasized concepts such as fairness, compassion, forgiveness, and obligation. These values influenced how communities understood justice and interpersonal responsibility. Over time, such principles became embedded in social customs and legal thinking, shaping how societies responded to wrongdoing and conflict.

Law and morality often develop together. While legal systems vary across cultures and historical periods, moral reasoning informed by Christianity contributed to how rules were justified and enforced. Ideas about right and wrong, duty and consequence, influenced both formal institutions and informal social regulation. Social norms reinforced moral behavior through shared expectations rather than constant enforcement. Individuals internalized moral standards through teaching, observation, and participation in community life.

Psychologically, this internalization reduced the

need for external control, as behavior came to be guided by a conscience shaped within a moral framework. These moral norms also shaped group identity. Belonging to a community meant understanding and adhering to shared values. Compliance reinforced acceptance, while deviation risked social disapproval. This dynamic strengthened cohesion but also highlighted the power of moral systems to include or exclude.

Christian moral frameworks contributed to the development of concepts of responsibility beyond the self. Individuals were encouraged to consider the impact of their actions on others and on the broader community. This outward focus supported prosocial behavior, reinforcing cooperation and mutual care. At the same time, moral systems are not neutral. Norms reflect the values of those who shape them, and moral authority can reinforce existing power structures. While Christian moral frameworks promoted social order, they also sometimes limited diversity of expression and justified conformity. These effects remain important to acknowledge.

Psychologically, moral clarity can reduce anxiety by offering guidance in complex situations. Knowing what is expected provides emotional reassurance. For many, Christian moral teachings served as a compass to guide decision-making and reduce uncertainty. However, moral rigidity can also create tension. When norms are applied rigidly or without context, they may provoke guilt, fear, or social pressure. These emotional consequences reveal the dual psychological impact of moral systems, both stabilizing and constraining.

Despite these tensions, moral frameworks

shaped by Christianity contributed to shared social understanding across generations. They provided continuity, reinforcing collective memory and shared expectations. This continuity supported long-term social stability. By influencing moral reasoning, laws, and social norms, Christianity played a significant role in structuring social life. These frameworks helped organize behavior and relationships, creating patterns that continue to influence societies today. Understanding this influence prepares us to examine how moral ideas about human worth and responsibility extended into broader discussions of dignity and rights.

Human Dignity And Women's Rights

Ideas about human dignity play a powerful role in shaping social life. They influence how people are valued, protected, and treated within communities. Christianity contributed to the development of moral language that emphasized the worth of the individual, framing human life as meaningful and morally significant within a larger social and ethical order.

From a psychological perspective, recognition of dignity supports self-worth and social belonging. When individuals are viewed as having inherent value, social relationships are shaped by responsibility rather than mere power. Christian teachings reinforced the idea that individuals mattered not only for their social role, but for their moral and relational significance.

These ideas influenced how societies gradually came to understand their responsibility toward others. Concepts such as care for the vulnerable, protection of the weak, and moral obligation beyond self-interest gained prominence within Christian moral frameworks. Over time, these values shaped social attitudes toward care, justice, and responsibility. Within this broader framework, Christianity also influenced discussions about women's social and moral status. While women's roles were often constrained by cultural norms, Christian moral teaching helped recognize women as moral agents within family and community life. This recognition shaped expectations of responsibility, dignity, and moral worth.

Psychologically, moral recognition affects identity. When individuals are acknowledged as capable of moral choice and responsibility, their sense of self is reinforced. Christian influence on women's moral identity contributed to how women understood themselves within social and relational roles, even when formal equality remained limited.

Christian teachings emphasized relational responsibility within families and communities. Women were often positioned as central figures in nurturing, moral instruction, and social continuity. These roles carried psychological significance, reinforcing identity, purpose, and responsibility within social structures.

At the same time, these contributions existed within patriarchal systems. While Christianity contributed to moral language about dignity, it did not dismantle existing gender hierarchies. Women's rights developed gradually and unevenly, shaped by social context as much as by religious belief. Acknowledging this tension is essential for an honest understanding. Social psychology reminds us that recognition and limitation can coexist. Individuals may experience affirmation within constrained systems. For many women, Christian communities offered belonging and purpose while also reinforcing boundaries that limited autonomy and authority.

Despite these limitations, the emphasis on human worth influenced later discussions of rights and responsibility. Moral language rooted in dignity contributed to evolving social expectations about care, protection, and ethical obligation toward women and other vulnerable groups.

Psychologically, dignity supports resilience. When individuals perceive their lives as meaningful and valued, they are better able to navigate hardship. Christian moral frameworks offered this psychological resource, reinforcing endurance and identity across generations. The development of women's rights cannot be attributed to Christianity alone, nor can it be separated entirely from it. Faith functioned as one among many influences, shaping moral discourse as it interacted with cultural, political, and social forces.

Understanding Christianity's contribution to ideas of human dignity and women's moral recognition helps explain both progress and limitation. These contributions laid the groundwork for subsequent discussions of equality and justice, while also revealing the complexity of belief within existing social structures. This balance prepares us to examine how education and knowledge further shape social and psychological development.

Education, Knowledge, And Social Advancement

Education plays a critical role in shaping both individual development and social structure. Christianity contributed to the spread and preservation of learning by emphasizing the importance of instruction, literacy, and moral formation. These contributions influenced how knowledge was valued and transmitted within societies over time.

From a psychological perspective, education supports cognitive development and social integration. Learning provides individuals with tools to understand the world and navigate social expectations. Christian institutions helped create structured environments in which knowledge could be taught, retained, and shared across generations.

Literacy was central to this process. The emphasis on sacred texts encouraged reading, interpretation, and teaching. Over time, this focus on literacy extended beyond religious instruction to encompass broader educational practices that fostered intellectual engagement and social participation. Educational settings shaped identity as well as knowledge. Schools and centers of learning influenced how individuals understood authority, discipline, and responsibility. These environments reinforced social norms while also fostering cognitive skills that supported reasoning and communication.

Christian involvement in education also contributed to continuity. Knowledge preserved through teaching helped societies maintain shared memory and cultural coherence. Psychologically, this continuity supported stability, offering individuals a sense of connection to a larger intellectual and moral tradition.

Education functioned as a pathway to social advancement. Access to learning expanded opportunities for participation in social and institutional life. While access was often unequal, the value placed on education influenced aspirations and social mobility within communities. Learning environments also reinforced moral and social values. Education was not viewed as a neutral transmission of information, but as the formation of character and responsibility. This approach shaped how individuals understood their role within society and their obligations to others.

At the social level, education supported innovation and organization. Knowledge facilitated administrative systems, communication, and social coordination. These developments contributed to societal functioning and long-term development, reinforcing the psychological benefits of order and structure. However, educational influence was shaped by power and access. Not all groups benefited equally from educational opportunities. While Christianity contributed to the preservation and spread of knowledge, it also reflected existing social hierarchies. These limitations remain important to acknowledge.

Psychologically, education provides a sense of competence and agency. When individuals acquire knowledge, they gain confidence in their ability to engage with the world. Christian educational efforts supported this sense of agency, reinforcing participation and responsibility. Education also shaped collective expectations. Societies influenced by Christian educational values often emphasized discipline, moral instruction, and intellectual engagement. These expectations shaped behavior and social interaction, reinforcing shared standards.

By contributing to education and knowledge transmission, Christianity influenced social advancement and psychological development. These contributions shaped how societies valued learning, responsibility, and progress. Understanding this influence prepares us to examine how faith further shaped family life, community care, and everyday social support.

Family, Community, And Social Care

Family and community structures play a vital role in shaping psychological well-being and social stability. Christianity influenced how societies understood family life, responsibility, and care for others. These influences shaped expectations about relationships, mutual obligation, and social support across generations. From a social psychological perspective, families provide the earliest context for identity formation.

Christian teachings reinforced the importance of family as a space for moral instruction, emotional support, and social continuity. Within this framework, family life became connected to values such as responsibility, care, and commitment.

Marriage and family relationships were often framed as moral and social responsibilities rather than purely personal choices. This framing shaped how individuals understood roles within the household and the broader community.

Psychologically, clear expectations provided structure and predictability, supporting stability in social relationships. Community life extended these values beyond the household. Christian communities functioned as networks of support, offering shared resources, guidance, and care. These communal structures reduced isolation and strengthened social bonds, particularly in times of hardship or crisis.

Charitable practices emerged as expressions of social responsibility. Caring for the poor, the sick, and the vulnerable became moral expectations within Christian-influenced societies. These practices reinforced empathy and prosocial behavior, contributing to collective well-being and psychological resilience. Social care was not limited to formal institutions. Informal support systems, shared labor, mutual aid, and community assistance played a vital role in daily life. These systems fostered trust and cooperation, reinforcing a sense of belonging and shared responsibility.

Psychologically, participation in care networks supports emotional health. When individuals feel supported and valued within a community, stress is reduced, and resilience is strengthened. Christian social structures contributed to these psychological benefits by emphasizing interconnectedness and mutual care. At the same time, family and community systems reflected social hierarchies. Roles within families and communities were often defined by gender, status, and tradition. While these structures provided stability for some, they also limited autonomy and reinforced inequality for others.

Social expectations surrounding family life shaped identity and behavior. Individuals were often evaluated based on conformity to established roles. This evaluation influenced self-worth and social standing, highlighting the dual psychological impact of a structure that is supportive for some, restrictive for others.

Despite these tensions, community care remained a significant contribution. In contexts where formal social systems were limited, religious communities provided essential support.

These networks helped individuals navigate loss, illness, and economic hardship, reinforcing survival and continuity. Family and community life also reinforced moral learning. Values were transmitted through daily interaction, shared rituals, and collective responsibility. Psychologically, this transmission supported socialization and internalization of norms that guided behavior.

By shaping family structures, community relationships, and social care practices, Christianity contributed to the psychological and social fabric of societies. These influences supported stability and mutual responsibility while also reflecting the limitations of their historical context. With this understanding, Chapter Four concludes, preparing us to examine how cultural dominance and social boundaries complicate these contributions in the chapters that follow.

Reflective Pause

✓ The contributions explored in this chapter reveal how Christianity functioned as a social and psychological resource for many individuals and communities. Through meaning, moral guidance, education, family life, and social care, faith helped shape structures that offered stability, belonging, and continuity across generations.

✓ For many, these influences supported emotional resilience and social cohesion. They provided language for responsibility, care, and purpose, helping people navigate uncertainty and hardship. At the same time, these contributions were shaped by historical context, power, and social norms that did not benefit everyone equally.

✓ As you pause, consider how support systems can also set limits. Reflect on how structure, expectations, and authority shape meaning and care. Positive influence does not require perfection, and contribution does not erase contradiction. Holding both realities together allows for a more honest understanding of how belief operates within society.

✓ This pause invites recognition, not celebration or dismissal, but awareness. Awareness of how faith has supported lives, and awareness of how the same structures can create boundaries that shape who belongs and how identity is defined.

The Bridge

The social and psychological contributions explored in this chapter did not exist in isolation. The same structures that fostered meaning, care, and stability also shaped cultural, social, and moral boundaries that defined inclusion and exclusion. As Christianity became more influential, its values and practices increasingly intersected with power, culture, and identity.

Chapter Five turns toward these boundaries. It examines how Christianity, when carried across cultures and societies, can sometimes reinforce dominance, suppress existing value systems, and reshape identity in ways that produce psychological strain. The focus shifts from contribution to consequence, from support to control, from cohesion to division.

This transition does not negate what has been explored so far. Instead, it deepens the conversation. Understanding contribution helps us better understand impact, and recognizing stability helps us see what is disrupted when boundaries harden.

As we move forward, the lens remains psychological and social. Chapter Five explores how belief, when aligned with power, can shape culture, identity, and belonging, often leaving lasting marks on individuals and communities.

CHAPTER FIVE

CULTURE, POWER, AND IDENTITY FORMATION

Christianity has never existed apart from culture. Wherever the faith has taken root, it has encountered societies already shaped by their own histories, values, moral systems, and spiritual traditions. These encounters were not neutral. They were shaped by power, by who defined truth, whose beliefs were affirmed, and whose ways of life were questioned, altered, or displaced.

This chapter examines how Christianity, when aligned with political, colonial, and cultural authority, profoundly influenced identity formation. It examines moments in which belief moved beyond spiritual teaching to become a force that reordered culture, reshaped self-understanding, and redefined belonging. The focus here is not on theology, but on the psychological and social consequences of power acting through belief.

In many contexts, particularly in Africa and other colonized societies. Christianity arrived not simply as a faith but as a cultural standard against which existing traditions were measured. Indigenous values, customs, and spiritual systems were often evaluated through foreign frameworks that positioned them as inferior or incompatible. These judgments carried psychological weight, shaping how individuals and communities understood themselves.

Culture is more than tradition; it is identity lived daily. It informs how people name their children, honor their ancestors, organize family life, interpret morality, and make sense of suffering and joy. When cultural systems are displaced rather than engaged, identity does not disappear; it fractures. This chapter examines how such fractures emerge and how they affect individuals' inner lives across generations.

Power plays a central role in this process. When belief is supported by authority, political, educational, or institutional, it gains the ability to define what is normal, acceptable, and valuable. This chapter will show how Christianity's alignment with power shaped cultural hierarchies and influenced which identities were affirmed and which were marginalized.

The discussion that follows moves carefully and deliberately. It does not present Christianity as a singular force with a single outcome, nor does it frame cultural encounter as universally destructive. Instead, it examines patterns, how dominance operates, how identity adapts under pressure, and how individuals negotiate belonging when belief challenges heritage.

This chapter also distinguishes culture from social regulation. While the next chapter will focus on gender, sexuality, and social boundaries, the focus here remains on culture and identity, on what happens when belief reshapes how people see their past, their values, and themselves.

By examining cultural encounter through the lens of power and psychology, this chapter invites readers to consider the emotional and identity-based consequences of religious dominance. These consequences are often subtle, unfolding over time, but their effects are enduring. The sections that follow explore cultural encounter, the displacement of African values, the treatment of Indigenous religions, the reinforcement of patriarchy, and the long-term fragmentation of identity. Together, they offer insight into how belief, when intertwined with power, can reshape not only societies but the inner worlds of those who live within them.

Cultural Encounter And Power

Christianity did not enter new societies as a neutral presence. It arrived in communities already shaped by long-standing cultural systems that ordered family life, morality, spirituality, and social responsibility. These encounters unfolded within unequal power relations, in which belief was often coupled with political authority, colonial influence, and institutional control. As a result, faith was experienced not only as spiritual teaching but as a cultural force.

Power shaped how Christianity was received and interpreted. In many contexts, Christian belief was presented as inseparable from Western cultural norms. Conversion implied more than acceptance of religious ideas; it required alignment with a new way of living, speaking, dressing, and understanding the world.

Culture and belief became intertwined in ways that privileged one system while diminishing another.

This imbalance influenced the psychological experience of belief. Indigenous communities were rarely invited to participate in equal dialogue. Their traditions were evaluated rather than understood, corrected rather than engaged. Christianity became associated with authority, while local cultures were framed as incomplete or misguided. Such framing reshaped how individuals perceived themselves within their own societies.

Power operates most effectively when it defines what is considered normal. When Christian norms were elevated as universal standards, difference was interpreted as a deficiency. Over time, individuals learned which behaviors brought approval and which invited correction. Identity formation occurred within these boundaries, shaping self-understanding through external validation. Cultural encounter extended into daily life. Language, education, and social institutions reinforced Christian norms as markers of progress and legitimacy. Participation in these systems often required cultural adjustment. Acceptance became conditional, reinforcing the idea that belonging depended on conformity.

Belief under these conditions was rarely a simple matter of conviction. Conversion often carried social and economic implications, influencing access to education, opportunity, and protection. Faith became intertwined with survival and advancement, complicating its psychological meaning. Acceptance offered security, while resistance carried cost. The dynamics of power help explain how this process took hold. **Michel Foucault** observed that *"power is everywhere; not because it embraces everything, but because it comes from everywhere."*

When belief is supported by authority embedded in institutions, education, and governance, it reshapes identity from within rather than relying solely on force.

Cultural encounters did not produce uniform outcomes. Individuals and communities responded in varied ways; some resisted, others adapted, and many negotiated complex paths between tradition and change. Identity formation under power involved compromise and tension rather than total submission or rejection.

Social psychology reminds us that identity depends on recognition. When one cultural system is affirmed and another dismissed, individuals experience uneven recognition. This imbalance affects self-worth and belonging long after the initial encounter, shaping emotional life and social behavior. Power also influences memory. Institutions associated with Christianity often controlled education and record-keeping, shaping which histories were preserved and which faded. Over time, dominant narratives became normalized, while alternative cultural memories were marginalized. Cultural encounter thus reshaped not only belief but also collective memory. The internalization of power makes domination enduring. **Steve Biko** warned that *"the most potent weapon in the hands of the oppressor is the mind of the oppressed."* When external standards become internal measures of worth, control no longer requires coercion; it becomes psychological.

These encounters laid the groundwork for deeper cultural displacement. Once the authority defined which ways of life were legitimate, it became easier to replace existing value systems rather than engage them. The next section examines this process, tracing how

African values were gradually displaced and how that displacement reshaped identity from within.

Displacement Of African Values

African societies carried value systems that shaped identity long before Christian contact. These values ordered family life, communal responsibility, moral conduct, and spiritual meaning. They lived their daily lives, as expressed through naming practices, rites of passage, respect for elders, communal labor, and shared moral expectations. Culture functioned as a framework for belonging, continuity, and self-understanding.

Displacement occurred when these value systems were no longer treated as meaningful in their own right. Rather than being engaged through dialogue, they were measured against foreign standards and gradually replaced. This process did not always appear forceful; it often unfolded quietly, reshaping daily life until what once felt natural came to feel unacceptable or inferior.

Names illustrate this process clearly. Traditional African names carried lineage, history, and moral aspiration. In many Christian contexts, these names were abandoned in favor of biblical or European ones. What appeared to be a spiritual gesture also carried psychological weight, signaling which histories were valued and which were meant to fade. Dress, music, and artistic expression followed a similar path. Cultural expressions central to African communal life were frequently labeled inappropriate or uncivilized. Over time, individuals learned to regulate how they expressed joy, grief, and identity. Cultural pride gave way to caution, and self-expression became something to manage rather than embody freely.

Moral values were also reshaped. African ethical systems emphasized communal responsibility, reciprocity, and shared accountability. These values supported social cohesion within tightly connected communities. When external moral frameworks were imposed without regard for local context, individuals were left to navigate competing systems of meaning: one inherited, the other institutionally rewarded. This tension did not always produce open conflict. More often, it produced ambivalence. People adapted outwardly while carrying quiet loss inwardly. Advancement became associated with cultural distance, teaching individuals, especially the young, that success required leaving parts of themselves behind.

The psychological depth of this process was captured by **Ngũgĩ wa Thiong'o**, who wrote that *"the domination of a people's language by the language of the colonizing nations was crucial to the domination of the mental universe of the colonized."* When language and culture are displaced, identity itself becomes unsettled.

Education played a significant role in reinforcing this shift. Schools often promoted foreign languages, values, and norms while discouraging Indigenous languages, values, and norms. Over time, children learned which cultural expressions were rewarded and which were corrected. This early socialization shaped self-concept and aspiration, embedding hierarchy into identity formation.

Family relationships were affected as well. Elders who carried cultural knowledge lost authority as younger generations aligned themselves with externally validated norms. This shift weakened intergenerational continuity, altering how wisdom, guidance, and identity were transmitted within families and communities. Cultural displacement also reshaped how people related to their past. Memory became selective. Traditions once passed on through story and practice were abandoned or forgotten. Identity became forward-looking but unanchored, oriented toward acceptance rather than continuity.

The Nigerian writer **Chinua Achebe** reflected on this kind of rupture when he wrote, *"the white man put a knife to the things that held us together, and we have fallen apart."* Displacement works in this way, not always through visible destruction, but through gradual separation from what once sustained coherence and belonging.

Displacement of African values did not erase meaning; it merely relocated where meaning was permitted to reside. Identity became something to negotiate rather than inherit. This internal negotiation laid the groundwork for deeper psychological division, particularly when spiritual traditions themselves were dismissed. The next section examines this dimension, assessing how Indigenous religions were treated and how spiritual invalidation intensified identity disruption.

Disdain For Indigenous Religions

Indigenous religions were not separate from daily life; they were woven into how people understood existence, morality, community, and the sacred. Spiritual beliefs shaped relationships with ancestors, guided communal rituals, and offered meaning during transitions such as birth, illness, and death. Religion functioned as a living system of knowledge, not merely a set of doctrines.

When Christianity encountered these spiritual traditions, the engagement was rarely mutual. Indigenous religions were often framed as primitive, superstitious, or morally corrupt. This framing created a hierarchy of belief in which one system was elevated to the status of truth while the other was dismissed as error. Such judgments extended beyond theology and entered the realm of identity.

Spiritual condemnation carries deep psychological weight. When a people's sacred traditions are labeled inferior or dangerous, belief becomes a source of shame rather than a source of grounding. Individuals are placed in a position where embracing a new faith requires rejecting the spiritual language that once gave coherence to their lives. This process was reinforced through instruction and socialization. Children were taught to associate ancestral practices with darkness or fear, while Christian belief was presented as enlightened and civilizing. Over time, emotional responses to spirituality were reshaped. Reverence gave way to caution, and curiosity was replaced by suspicion.

Conversion under these conditions involved rupture. Individuals were encouraged to sever ties with ancestral rituals, sacred spaces, and spiritual authorities. What was framed as spiritual progress often involved loss, loss of continuity between generations, and loss of connection to inherited meaning. African philosophy emphasizes the inseparability of spirituality and community. **Placide Tempels** expressed this when he wrote that *"for the Bantu, religion, morals, and law are not separate domains but form a single reality."* When Indigenous religion was dismissed, it was not only belief that was rejected, but an entire way of organizing life.

Spiritual invalidation also reshaped moral understanding. Practices once interpreted as expressions of reverence were redefined as sinful or threatening. Individuals were left to navigate conflicting moral worlds: one rooted in inherited tradition, the other enforced by religious authority.

Communal life suffered as a result. Sacred rituals that once unified communities were abandoned or driven underground. Spiritual leaders lost influence, and shared symbols lost meaning. The weakening of collective spiritual practice disrupted how communities processed grief, healing, and social transition. The philosopher **Sophie Oluwole** warned of this loss when she observed that *"to destroy a people's religion is to destroy their system of meaning and understanding."* Spiritual displacement erodes more than belief; it removes interpretive tools that once sustained emotional and psychological resilience.

For many individuals, spirituality became divided. Christian worship occupied public space, while ancestral belief retreated into silence or secrecy. This division produced a fragmented spiritual identity, in which parts of the self were affirmed while others were concealed. Such fragmentation shaped experiences of authenticity and belonging. Over time, fear replaced familiarity. Spirituality became associated with obedience rather than relationship, rule rather than rhythm. Emotional distance replaced the sacred intimacy, altering how individuals experienced faith and devotion.

The disdain for Indigenous religions intensified the identity disruption already produced by cultural displacement. When both culture and spirituality are delegitimized, the self loses stable grounding. This dynamic set the stage for further hierarchies, particularly gendered power structures, which become more visible in the next section's exploration of patriarchy and male superiority.

Patriarchy And Male Superiority

Gender hierarchy existed in many societies prior to Christian contact, shaped by tradition, economics, and social organization. When Christianity entered these contexts, it often aligned with existing patriarchal structures rather than challenging them. Religious authority became another channel through which male dominance was reinforced and normalized.

Interpretations of Christian teaching frequently emphasized male leadership and female submission. These interpretations were presented not as cultural arrangements, but as moral or spiritual order. When hierarchy is framed as sacred, it becomes resistant to question, shaping how power is understood and accepted within everyday life.

Psychologically, sacred authority carries unique weight. When gender roles are justified through belief, they are internalized as moral expectations rather than social constructs. Women are not only excluded from authority; they are also taught to regard limitation as a virtue. This internalization influences self-concept, confidence, and emotional well-being.

Religious institutions reinforced these patterns through their structures and practices. Leadership roles were overwhelmingly held by men, establishing a visible link between authority and masculinity. Communities learned who was meant to speak, decide, and lead through repeated observation. Over time, these patterns became familiar, even unquestioned.

Family life mirrored institutional norms. Teachings on male headship and female submission shaped household expectations. While these roles offered structure for some families, they also constrained women's autonomy and decision-making. Psychological security became tied to compliance rather than mutual agency.

Education and religious instruction further shaped gender identity. Women were often directed toward roles centered on caregiving, modesty, and service, while men were positioned as decision-makers and moral authorities. These expectations shaped aspiration, subtly limiting how women imagined their futures.

The feminist philosopher **Simone de Beauvoir**

captured the psychological roots of this dynamic when she wrote, *"One is not born, but rather becomes, a woman."* Gender roles reinforced through belief are learned and repeated, shaping identity through social expectation rather than biology alone.

Male superiority also operated through moral scrutiny. Women's behavior was more closely monitored, particularly in matters of sexuality and obedience. Unequal scrutiny produced emotional consequences, shaping experiences of guilt, shame, and fear in gendered ways. Men, too, were shaped by these norms. Masculinity became associated with control, authority, and emotional restraint. While men benefited from privilege, they were also confined by rigid roles that discouraged vulnerability and emotional expression. Patriarchy constrains human experience at both ends of the hierarchy.

Power persists through repetition. When gender hierarchy is continually presented as natural or divinely ordered, it becomes difficult to imagine alternatives. Social psychology shows that norms repeated across institutions become internalized, shaping belief even in the absence of enforcement.

The theologian **Mary Daly** warned of this effect when she wrote, *"If God is male, then the male is God."* When religious language centers male authority, it shapes not only institutions but consciousness itself, reinforcing hierarchy at the level of thought. The reinforcement of male superiority did not exist in isolation. It is intersected with cultural displacement and spiritual invalidation already explored in this chapter. As traditional systems were weakened, Christian institutions often filled the void, bringing gender norms shaped by foreign contexts but enforced through religious authority. These dynamics prepare the way for the broader system of social boundaries to be examined in the next chapter.

Identity Fragmentation

Identity is not formed in isolation. It develops through culture, belief, memory, and belonging. When these foundations are disrupted, identity does not simply adapt; it fragments. Fragmentation occurs when individuals are required to live between worlds, carrying pieces of self that no longer fit comfortably together.

The processes explored throughout this chapter, unequal cultural encounter, displacement of values, spiritual invalidation, and gender hierarchy, did not operate independently. Together, they reshaped how individuals understood who they were, where they belonged, and which parts of themselves were acceptable. Identity became something to manage rather than something to inhabit. For many, this fragmentation was subtle. It appeared as an unspoken tension between public and private life. Christian belief occupied visible space, while cultural memory retreated into silence. Individuals learned to present one version of themselves in religious and institutional settings, while holding another version quietly within.

This divided self-carried a psychological cost. When parts of identity are consistently corrected, hidden, or devalued, individuals experience inner conflict. Belonging becomes conditional. Self-worth becomes fragile, dependent on approval rather than rooted in continuity. Over time, this instability shapes emotional life, producing anxiety, guilt, and uncertainty.

Language often reflected this fragmentation. Words associated with culture and tradition were replaced or avoided. Spiritual language shifted away from ancestral meaning toward externally defined frameworks. Thought itself became divided, shaped by competing value systems that did not easily reconcile. Generational transmission intensified the effect. Children inherited identities shaped by loss they did not personally experience but nonetheless carried. Cultural disconnection became normalized, even when its emotional roots were not fully understood. What was lost could not always be named, yet its absence was felt.

Identity fragmentation also affected belonging. Individuals moved through institutions that rewarded conformity while quietly distancing them from cultural origins. Community became conditional, tied to adherence rather than wholeness. Belonging was granted, but often at the cost of internal division.

Psychologically, fragmentation weakens coherence. When identity lacks integration, individuals struggle to feel grounded. Decision-making becomes fraught, as choices feel like betrayals of one part of the self in favor of another. This tension does not resolve easily; it becomes a lived experience. Spiritual fragmentation compounded this struggle. Faith, once a source of meaning, became intertwined with loss. Individuals learned to associate spiritual belonging with a sense of separation from cultural roots. This association reshaped emotional responses to belief, introducing ambivalence where there might otherwise have been clarity.

Gendered expectations further complicated identity. Women navigating patriarchal norms faced more layers of fragmentation, balancing cultural memory, religious expectation, and personal agency. Men, too, carried fragmented identities shaped by rigid definitions of authority and restraint.

Over time, fragmentation became normalized. Living between identities felt ordinary, even expected. Yet normalization does not erase impact. The psychological effort needed to maintain divided selves accumulates, shaping self-concept, relationships, and emotional health.

Identity fragmentation does not imply the absence of meaning. Individuals found ways to survive, adapt, and create coherence within constraints. But survival under fragmentation is not the same as wholeness. Understanding this distinction is essential to grasping the long-term psychological consequences of belief shaped by power.

This chapter has traced how culture, authority, and belief interact to reshape identity. Fragmentation appears not from belief alone, but from belief enforced through dominance. These dynamics set the stage for the next chapter, in which attention shifts from cultural identity to social regulation, examining how boundaries around gender, sexuality, and belonging continue to shape who is included and who is still at the margins.

Reflective Pause

✓ Culture shapes identity quietly. It lives in language, memory, gesture, and belonging long before it is named. When belief enters culture through power, it does more than teach; it reshapes how people understand themselves and their place in the world.

✓ The experiences explored in this chapter reveal how identity can be reshaped without being fully erased. What is displaced does not disappear; it lingers in memory, emotion, and inherited silence. People learn to live with divided selves, carrying faith in one hand and loss in the other.

✓ For some, this tension becomes normal. For others, it stays a source of quiet discomfort. Either way, it shapes how individuals relate to community, spirituality, and self-worth. Cultural memory may fade, but its absence continues to speak.

✓ This pause is not an invitation to blame or defend. It is an invitation to notice. To recognize how power leaves psychological traces that persist beyond history. To acknowledge that belief can offer meaning while also requiring sacrifice, sometimes of parts of the self that once felt whole.

✓ As you pause here, consider how identity is shaped by what is affirmed and what is corrected. Reflect on what it means to belong without fragmentation, and what it costs when belonging is conditional. These reflections prepare the ground for the next chapter, where attention turns to social boundaries that continue to shape inclusion and exclusion in everyday life.

The Bridge

The effects of culture and power do not remain confined to the inner life. The identity fragmentation explored in this chapter finds expression in social structures, rules, expectations, and norms that shape who belongs and who does not. What begins as cultural disruption becomes social regulation.

As belief aligns with authority, it moves beyond shaping identity to define boundaries. These boundaries determine acceptable roles, behaviors, and relationships. They organize society by drawing lines between male and female, moral and immoral, acceptable, and unacceptable. Over time, these distinctions harden, shaping everyday life.

The psychological consequences of such boundaries are significant. When social norms are framed as sacred or unchangeable, they gain emotional force. Compliance becomes associated with virtue, while deviation carries stigma. Belonging becomes conditional, and difference is often interpreted as failure rather than variation.

Chapter Six turns toward these boundaries. It examines how Christianity has influenced social definitions of gender, sexuality, and moral legitimacy, shaping who is affirmed and who is marginalized. The focus shifts from cultural encounter to social control, from inherited identity to regulated behavior.

This transition does not abandon the themes explored so far. Instead, it extends them. The same forces that reshaped culture and identity also shaped social expectations, reinforcing hierarchies that continue to affect lives today. Understanding these boundaries requires attention not only to belief, but to the psychological weight of inclusion and exclusion.

As the discussion progresses, the question shifts from the loss of culture to the constraints on life. The next chapter explores how social boundaries are constructed, enforced, and internalized, and how they continue to shape human experience in profound ways.

CHAPTER SIX

SOCIAL BOUNDARIES

Belief does more than shape personal conviction; it organizes social life. As Christianity gained influence within societies, it contributed to the formation of moral, social, and relational boundaries that defined who belonged, how people were expected to live, and which identities were affirmed or restricted. These boundaries did not exist only in doctrine; they were lived daily, enforced through norms, expectations, and social judgment.

This chapter explores how Christianity has shaped social boundaries and the psychological consequences of those boundaries. It examines how belief, when tied to authority, regulates behavior and identity, particularly in areas related to gender, sexuality, and moral legitimacy. The focus is not on belief as private faith, but on belief as a social structure. Boundaries serve a social function. They create order, provide clarity, and establish shared expectations. At the same time, they also exclude. When moral boundaries are framed as sacred or absolute, deviation becomes more than difference; it becomes failure. Belonging becomes conditional, and identity is evaluated through conformity.

Social psychology helps us understand how these processes work. Shame, guilt, fear of rejection, and desire for acceptance become powerful regulatory tools. Individuals learn what is permissible not only through instruction, but through observation, who is affirmed, who is corrected, and who is silenced. Over time, these patterns shape self-concept and emotional life. This chapter turns its attention to those who live at or beyond these boundaries. It also examines how women's roles have been regulated, how sexuality has been morally defined, and how queer people identities have been positioned within Christian moral frameworks. It also considers the psychological consequences of exclusion, the internalization of stigma, and the negotiation of identity under pressure.

The discussion does not assume uniform experience. Social boundaries are enforced differently across cultures and communities. Some individuals comply outwardly while struggling inwardly; others resist, reinterpret, or redefine belonging. These varied responses reveal the complexity of belief as both constraint and a coping mechanism.

This chapter examines how social boundaries are constructed, supported, and internalized. It will also explore moments of resistance, in which individuals and communities push back against restrictive norms to pursue dignity, agency, and belonging. By focusing on social boundaries, this chapter extends the conversation begun in earlier chapters. Cultural disruption and identity fragmentation do not remain internal experiences; they surface in social rules that govern bodies, relationships, and expression. Understanding these boundaries allows for a deeper examination of how belief continues to shape psychological experience in everyday life.

What follows is an exploration of inclusion and exclusion, not to assign blame or offer simple solutions, but to illuminate how social boundaries affect human lives. Through this lens, the chapter invites readers to reflect on the cost of belonging when it is conditioned, and the resilience required to live authentically within or beyond the lines drawn by belief.

Social Boundaries And Moral Regulation

Social boundaries are the lines societies draw to define acceptable behavior, identity, and belonging. Within Christian-influenced contexts, these boundaries have often been shaped by moral teachings that extend beyond personal conviction to collective expectations. Belief functions as a social organizer, guiding how people are expected to live, relate, and present themselves within the community. Moral regulation operates most effectively when it is normalized. Rather than relying on constant enforcement, societies cultivate shared understandings of right and wrong that individuals internalize over time. Christianity contributed to these shared moral frameworks, shaping behavior through teaching, ritual, and social reinforcement.

From a psychological perspective, moral boundaries are maintained through emotional mechanisms. Shame, guilt, and fear of disapproval function as powerful regulators of behavior. Individuals learn not only what is expected, but what must be avoided to preserve belonging and social acceptance.

Belonging is central to this process. Communities offer connection, support, and meaning, but often at a cost. Acceptance becomes conditional on adherence to moral norms. When conformity is rewarded and deviation punished, individuals learn to monitor themselves, adjusting behavior to remain within accepted boundaries.

Moral regulation extends into everyday life. Dress, speech, relationships, and expressions of identity are evaluated against religiously informed norms. These evaluations may not always be explicit, but they are felt through social cues, approval, correction, silence, or exclusion.

The sociologist **Émile Durkheim** observed that *"society can exist only if there is among its members a sufficient degree of homogeneity."* Moral boundaries help create this homogeneity, but they also narrow the range of acceptable difference. Psychological safety is associated with sameness rather than authenticity. Religious authority strengthens moral regulation by framing norms as sacred. When expectations are presented as divinely sanctioned, questioning them feels not only risky but morally wrong. This framing intensifies emotional compliance, shaping conscience as much as conduct.

Internalization is key. Over time, individuals no longer need external enforcement to regulate behavior. Moral standards have become part of self-identity. This internalization creates order, but it also increases the psychological cost of deviation. Breaking norms can feel like self-betrayal and social transgression. Social boundaries are not applied equally. Those with less power experience stricter regulation and harsher consequences. Marginalized groups are more closely monitored, while dominant groups often enjoy greater flexibility. This uneven application reveals how moral boundaries reinforce existing hierarchies.

The philosopher **Michel Foucault** captured this dynamic when he wrote, *"discipline produces subjected and practiced bodies."* Moral regulation shapes not only belief but behavior, teaching individuals how to move, speak, and exist within socially acceptable limits. For many, moral boundaries provide clarity and structure. They reduce uncertainty and offer guidance for navigating complex social life. Yet the same boundaries can produce anxiety and fear when individuals feel they cannot fully conform. The psychological burden of constant self-regulation accumulates over time.

Understanding moral regulation helps explain how social boundaries take hold and endure. These boundaries prepare the ground for more specific forms of control, particularly around gender and sexuality. The next section examines these dynamics, tracing how women's lives and bodies have been regulated within Christian moral frameworks.

Gender Roles And The Regulation Of Women

Across societies influenced by Christianity, women's lives have often been shaped by moral expectations that extend beyond personal belief into social regulation. These expectations defined appropriate behavior, roles, and visibility, framing womanhood through ideals of obedience, modesty, and self-sacrifice. Gender became not only a social category but a moral one. In fact, religious teaching played a significant role in shaping these expectations. Interpretations of Christian doctrine emphasized order and hierarchy, positioning men as leaders and women as supporters. These arrangements were presented as natural or divinely intended, lending moral authority to social structures that limited women's autonomy.

Psychologically, moral framing carries particular weight. When gender roles are tied to virtue, deviation is experienced not merely as difference but as moral failure. Women learn early which behaviors are praised and which are corrected, shaping self-awareness through constant evaluation. Social regulation operates through repetition. Expectations are reinforced through sermons, family norms, education, and community life. Over time, these patterns become familiar, shaping identity without requiring overt enforcement. Regulation becomes internal, guiding behavior through conscience rather than command.

Women's bodies became central sites of moral regulation. Standards of dress, sexuality, and appearance were closely monitored, often justified as expressions of purity or respectability. These standards placed disproportionate responsibility for maintaining the moral order on women, linking their behavior to communal virtue. This regulation shaped emotional life. Fear of judgment, shame, and self-doubt became common psychological companions. Many women learned to measure their worth through compliance, equating acceptance with moral success and rejection with personal failure.

Family life reflected these dynamics. Teachings on submission and headship shaped expectations within marriage and household roles. While some women found meaning and identity within these frameworks, others experienced constraints and silencing, unable to express agency without social consequences. Education reinforced these patterns. Religious instruction often emphasized virtues associated with restraint and service for women, while leadership and authority were associated with men. These messages shaped aspiration, influencing how women imagined their futures and their place in the world.

The philosopher **Simone de Beauvoir** captured the learned nature of gender roles when she wrote, *"One is not born, but rather becomes, a woman."* This insight reflects how social expectations, reinforced through belief, shape identity over time, teaching women how to inhabit roles assigned rather than chosen. Social boundaries surrounding womanhood were not uniform. Class, race, and cultural context influenced how regulation was experienced.

Some women navigated these boundaries with relative freedom, while others faced stricter control and harsher judgment. Power shaped whose conformity mattered most. Resistance often took subtle forms. Women negotiated expectations quietly, adapting roles to preserve dignity and agency. Such resistance rarely appeared as open defiance; instead, it emerged through reinterpretation, silence, or selective compliance. Yet even quiet resistance carried a psychological cost. Navigating between expectation and self-understanding required constant emotional labor. The effort to belong without erasing oneself produced fatigue, ambivalence, and inner conflict.

The regulation of women also influenced how communities understood morality itself. Virtue became gendered, associated with female behavior rather than male conduct. This imbalance reinforced inequality, normalizing scrutiny of women while excusing or overlooking male transgression.

Understanding how gender roles were regulated within Christian contexts reveals how social boundaries operate through belief. These boundaries shaped not only women's opportunities, but their inner lives, how they understood worth, voice, and belonging. This dynamic prepares us to examine how similar moral regulation extends the Psychological impact of moral exclusion on sexuality and LGBTQI+ identities in the next section.

The Psychological Impact Of Moral Exclusion On Sexuality And Lgbtqi+ Identities

Sexuality has long been a central site of moral regulation within Christian-influenced societies. This moral shaped not only how relationships were understood, but how desire itself was viewed. Sexual behavior became closely tied to ideas of morality, purity, and social order, positioning certain identities as acceptable and others as transgressive. Within the Christian community, sexuality is seen through strict binaries of right and wrong. Heterosexual marriages were upheld as the normative ideal. In other words, the heterosexual marriage is a union that is meant for a man and a woman as a result of God covenantal blessings of procreation, while other forms of sexual identity and expression were considered sinful, disordered, or morally dangerous.

These verdicts did not remain abstract; they shaped how individuals were treated within families, churches, schools, and the at large communities. The truth is that the definition of marriage has been challenged by the legal recognition of queer marriages in several nations. This development has sparked global debates concerning morality, human rights, and religious freedom. However, as a Christian psychologist there should be a ministerial response and community engagement.

Psychologically, the harsh condemnation of identity carries deep consequences. When a person's sense of self is framed as morally wrong, rejection is experienced not as disagreement but as negation, without a proper understanding of why an individual behaves or acts the way they act. Different research found out how LGBTQI+ individuals are often encountered with the messages that required them to choose between authenticity and belonging. Moral regulation extended beyond behavior to identity itself. One particular respondent said, *"identity was not merely discouraged; it was often denied legitimacy."* In other words, individuals were encouraged to suppress, conceal, or alter aspects of themselves to remain within accepted boundaries.

Biblically, the scripture did not encourage any form of exclusion, rather it teaches how to live with one another. The queer individuals or group are not the people that we can run away from or harshly condemned. Love is the reason for accepting and understanding anyone practicing LGBTQ+ just as God loves everyone (1 Peter 4:8). It is important to have compassion about those into it, listening to their experiences and struggles, and seeking to understand their perspectives (Colossians 3:12-14). Christian must make such that the queer individuals are not a cast away, there is need for showing hospitality, creating a welcoming environment for everyone to feel valued and accepted even with their background or identity (Romans 15:7).

Shame functioned as a primary mechanism of control. Fear of exposure, judgment, or exclusion shaped emotional life negatively. Many learned to monitor their thoughts, language, and relationships carefully, internalizing vigilance as a form of survival which often leads to pretense. Religious teaching intensified this experience by framing moral boundaries as divinely ordained.

Questioning these boundaries was not simply social risk; it was harshly presented as spiritual rebellion. This framing made internal conflict especially painful, as doubt became entangled with fear of moral failure. Theologian **James Cone** once observed that *"any theology that does not take the suffering of the oppressed seriously is not Christian theology."* For LGBTQI+ individuals, moral condemnation translated into lived suffering, rejection, isolation, and spiritual alienation, experienced not as abstraction but as daily reality.

Family relationships often became sites of tension. Acceptance within the home was frequently conditional, shaped by religious expectation. Some individuals were pressured to conform; others were silenced; and many distanced themselves from those they loved to protect their emotional safety. Church communities reinforced these boundaries through teaching and practice. LGBTQI + identities were often discussed in moral terms without the presence or voices of those affected. Silence became both a strategy of survival and a marker of exclusion. The Church communities response to sexuality and LGBTQI+ identities must be characterized by both conviction and compassion just as Jesus consistently demonstrated love toward sinners. Of course, moral teaching must always be redemptive, aiming to restore broken people to God and not condemnations.

The psychological burden of concealment accumulated over time. Living with a divided identity, one self-visible, another hidden, produced anxiety and emotional exhaustion. Authenticity felt dangerous, while belonging felt contingent and fragile. Not all responses followed the same path. Some individuals internalized condemnation, directing blame inward. Others rejected religious affiliation altogether, separating faith from survival. Still others sought reinterpretation, attempting to reconcile belief with lived experience. Social psychology highlights how exclusion shapes self-concept. Persistent stigma influences how individuals see themselves, often leading to internalized shame and diminished self-worth. When rejection is framed as moral truth, its effects are particularly enduring.

The regulation of sexuality also affected broader social attitudes. LGBTQI+ identities became symbols of moral threat in family, church, school, and the community at large-reinforcing fear and misunderstanding. These narratives justified exclusion while masking the human cost beneath moral language. Here are three suggested Christian psychological response to sexuality and LGBTQ+ identities.

1. **Develop a Compassionate Response:** By listening and understanding the person, creating an atmosphere for interaction that leads to showing love and hospitality that will make anyone in that situation feel that they are appreciated.

2. **Building Relationships and Partnerships:** Building bridges between LGBTQ+ individuals and faith communities is not an easy task, because this involves two different parties. The only way to work together with two different mind sets is by coherence. However, "*we recognize the diversity and critical within-group differences when teaching about sexual orientation, gender diversity, and LGBTQ psychology*". (Burnes and Stanley, 2017, 10) Understanding the LGBTQ+ is an approach to design the method of building relationship in the society and it involves psychology. Psychology of LGBTQ+ implies the study of behavior of LGBTQ+ people, their beliefs, and the mental processes.

3. **Fostering a Culture of Inclusivity:** Corporate worship creates inclusive spaces and practices for encouraging people toward more theological, emotional, and Christ-exalting engagement. As stated by Merker "*above all, he keeps us focused on Jesus Christ, the one in*

whose name we gather, and whose substitutionary death and victorious resurrection are the reason we worship" (Merker 2021, 5). In such gathering, everyone needs to focus on the God by listening to His word, not a place of discrimination, condemnation and critiquing one and another. Even, if queer individuals feels shy and dejected, fellow Christians or leader should embrace the person letting them know how God loves everyone. Such gathering must be encouraging empathy, compassion, and love in all interactions. No element of class should be portrayed indicating superstar. A place that is conducive for worship is mixed with both Christian and wayward, most important Christ is glorified.

Understanding how sexuality has been regulated within Christian moral frameworks reveals the depth of the social boundaries shaped by belief. These boundaries have determined who could belong openly and who was required to remain hidden, who was affirmed, and who was marked as morally suspect. Before turning to the psychological consequences of exclusion itself, it is important to pause and listen to voices that have named these experiences across history and culture, voices that speak to dignity, silence, resistance, and the human cost of enforced boundaries. Their words do not interrupt this conversation; they deepen it, preparing us to examine how stigma and exclusion affect the inner life in the following section.

Voices On Boundaries, Identity, And Belonging

Before continuing, it is important to pause and listen.

The social boundaries explored in this chapter, around gender, sexuality, morality, and belonging, have long been named and challenged by voices across history, faith, politics, and culture. These voices do not speak in one register, nor do they share identical convictions. What unites them is a shared recognition of human dignity and the psychological cost of exclusion. The quotations that follow are not arguments. They are witnesses. They give language to experiences of marginalization, silence, moral judgment, and resilience. Placed here, they prepare the reader to enter the next section with attentiveness to the human realities that live beneath social rules and moral systems.

On Human Dignity and Equality

- ✓ **Nelson Mandela -** *"To deny people their human rights is to challenge their very humanity."*
- ✓ **President Barack Obama -** *"We are all born equal, but we are not treated equally."*
- ✓ **Mahatma Gandhi -** *"A nation's greatness is measured by how it treats its weakest members."*
- ✓ **Cornel West -** *"Justice is what love looks like in public."*

On Power, Oppression, and Moral Authority

- ✓ **Desmond Tutu -** *"If you are neutral in situations of injustice, you have chosen the side of the oppressor."*
- ✓ **President Olusegun Obasanjo -** *"Leadership is about*

responsibility, not privilege."
- ✓ **Alice Walker** - *"The most common way people give up their power is by thinking they don't have any."*
- ✓ **Bell Hooks** - *"Oppression is not only about the absence of choice, but the presence of coercion."*

On Gender, Identity, and Internalized Hierarchy

- ✓ **Simone de Beauvoir** - *"When an individual is kept in a position of inferiority, the fact is that he does become inferior."*
- ✓ **Mary Daly** - *"If God is male, then the male is God."*
- ✓ **Audre Lorde** - *"I am not free while any woman is unfree, even when her shackles are very different from my own."*

On Exclusion, Silence, and Psychological Harm

- ✓ **James Baldwin** - *"To be rejected by one's own community is one of the deepest forms of human suffering."*
- ✓ **Maya Angelou** - *"There is no greater agony than bearing an untold story inside you."*
- ✓ **Brené Brown** - *"Shame is the most powerful, master emotion. It's the fear that we're not worthy of connection."*
- ✓ **Elie Wiesel** - *"What hurts the victim most is not the cruelty of the oppressor but the silence of the bystander."*
- ✓ **Erich Fromm** - *"The price of conformity is the erosion of the self."*

On Faith, Judgment, and Moral Boundaries

- ✓ **Pope Francis** - *"We are all sinners. Who am I to judge?"*
- ✓ **Bishop T.D. Jakes** - *"You can't heal what you won't*

confront."

On Voice, Resistance, and the Possibility of Change

- ✓ **Oprah Winfrey -** *"What I know for sure is that speaking your truth is the most powerful tool we all have."*
- ✓ **First Lady Michelle Obama -** *"When they go low, we go high."*
- ✓ **Toni Morrison -** *"The function of freedom is to free someone else."*
- ✓ **Martin Luther King Jr. -** *"We know through painful experience that freedom is never voluntarily given by the oppressor; it must be demanded by the oppressed."*
- ✓ **Frederick Douglass -** *"It is easier to build strong children than to repair broken men."*

Why These Voices Appear Here

This collection is placed intentionally at this point in the chapter.

The sections preceding this pause examined how social boundaries are constructed through belief, moral regulation, gender norms, and sexual condemnation. The following section examines how those boundaries affect the human psyche: stigma, shame, exclusion, and psychological harm.

These voices stand between structure and consequence. They remind us that beneath doctrine, policy, and moral language are lived human experiences, fear, silence, resistance, resilience, and the longing to belong without leisure. They prepare the reader not only to understand but also to empathize.

This pause is not meant to resolve tension. It is meant to honor reality.

What follows will examine the psychological consequences of exclusion in greater depth. These voices prepare the reader to enter that discussion with attentiveness, empathy, and honesty.

Exclusion, Stigma, And Psychological Consequences

Exclusion is not only a social condition but also a psychological experience. When individuals are pushed beyond accepted boundaries, the impact reaches inward, shaping how they understand themselves and their place in the world. Stigma does not remain external; it settles into thought, emotion, and self-perception.

Stigma functions by marking difference as deficiency. It labels certain identities, behaviors, or experiences as undesirable, unworthy, or morally suspect. Once attached, stigma follows individuals across social spaces, shaping how they are perceived and how they come to perceive themselves.

The emotional effects of exclusion are often immediate. Rejection triggers fear, grief, and confusion. Over time, these emotions can harden into chronic stress, anxiety, or despair. The need to belong is fundamental to human psychology; when belonging is denied, emotional stability is threatened.

Shame plays a central role in this process. Unlike guilt, which is tied to behavior, shame targets identity. It communicates that something is wrong, not with what a person does, but with who they are. This distinction makes shame particularly damaging, as it undermines self-worth at its core.

Social exclusion also reshapes behavior. Individuals learn to avoid attention, suppress expression, and anticipate judgment. Self-monitoring becomes habitual. Silence becomes a protective strategy. Over time, these adaptations can limit emotional expression and reduce a sense of authenticity.

The sociologist **Erving Goffman** described stigma as *"an attribute that is deeply discrediting,"* noting that it reduces a person *"from a whole and usual person to a tainted, discounted one."* This description captures how stigma simultaneously alters social interaction and internal identity.

Exclusion affects relationships as well. Trust becomes difficult when acceptance feels conditional. Individuals may withdraw to protect themselves from further harm, resulting in isolation that compounds psychological distress. Even within supportive spaces, the fear of rejection can linger.

Mental health consequences often emerge gradually. Persistent exposure to stigma increases vulnerability to depression, anxiety, and emotional exhaustion. The effort required to navigate hostile or judgmental environments drains psychological resources, leaving individuals fatigued and disconnected.

For those excluded on moral or religious grounds, the impact can be especially complex. When rejection is framed as spiritual truth, individuals may struggle to separate social judgment from divine judgment. This confusion intensifies inner conflict, blending emotional pain with spiritual fear.

Exclusion also shapes identity development. Individuals may internalize negative labels, adjusting their self-concept to align with their treatment. Others resist internalization, but resistance itself requires strength and constant effort. Either path carries emotional cost.

Community response matters deeply. When exclusion is reinforced by silence or complicity, harm is amplified. Conversely, moments of recognition, like being seen, believed, or affirmed, can interrupt the cycle of stigma. Psychological healing often begins with a restoration of dignity.

Social psychology reminds us that stigma is sustained through shared narratives. When stories about certain groups emphasize danger, immorality, or deficiency, exclusion becomes justified. Challenging stigma, therefore, requires changing not only attitudes, but the stories societies tell about belonging.

Exclusion is not experienced equally. Intersecting identities, such as gender, race, sexuality, and class, shape how stigma is felt and enforced. Some individuals face layered exclusion, intensifying psychological vulnerability and limiting access to support.

Understanding the psychological consequences of exclusion reveals why social boundaries matter. They do not simply organize society; they shape emotional life, self-worth, and mental health. This understanding prepares us to examine how individuals and communities respond, through resistance, reinterpretation, and the search for belonging, explored in the final section of this chapter.

Belonging, Resistance, And Re-Negotiation

Belonging is a fundamental human need. It provides emotional security, identity, and a sense of place within the social world. When belonging is threatened or denied, individuals do not simply withdraw; they adapt, resist, and renegotiate their existence within or outside the boundaries imposed upon them.

Resistance does not always take visible or confrontational forms. For many, it begins quietly, through internal questioning, reinterpretation of belief, or selective participation. Individuals learn to navigate social expectations in ways that preserve dignity while minimizing risk. This form of resistance is often invisible, yet psychologically significant.

Re-negotiation occurs when individuals seek to redefine the terms of belonging. Rather than accepting exclusion outright, they explore new meanings of faith, community, and self-worth. This process allows continuity without total conformity, enabling people to remain connected without erasing their identities.

Belief itself becomes a site of reinterpretation. Some individuals revisit religious teachings through alternative lenses, separating core spiritual values from institutional enforcement. In doing so, faith becomes less about regulation and more about meaning, compassion, and personal conscience. Community plays a critical role in this process. New forms of belonging often emerge at the margins, such as support groups, affirming faith spaces, chosen families, and informal networks. These communities offer recognition where traditional structures have failed, restoring a sense of visibility and value.

Psychologically, resistance strengthens agency. It allows individuals to move from passive endurance to intentional self-definition. Even small acts of self-assertion, speaking openly, setting boundaries, and choosing authenticity can disrupt the internalized effects of stigma. Belonging, when renegotiated, becomes less conditional. Rather than depending solely on conformity, it is rooted in mutual recognition and shared humanity.

This shift reduces the emotional cost of participation, allowing individuals to engage without constant self-surveillance. Not all resistance leads to reconciliation. Some individuals choose to distance themselves from religious institutions altogether. This decision is not always a rejection of faith, but a response to harm. Psychological well-being sometimes requires separation from environments that consistently undermine self-worth. Re-negotiation also involves grief. Letting go of familiar structures, beliefs, communities, and identities can be painful. Loss accompanies transformation, even when change leads toward healing. Acknowledging this grief is essential to understanding the emotional complexity of resistance.

The psychologist **Carl Rogers** captured the importance of authenticity when he wrote, *"The curious paradox is that when I accept myself just as I am, then I can change."* Acceptance becomes the foundation for growth, not conformity. Belonging rooted in authenticity fosters resilience. When individuals are seen and affirmed, they regain emotional stability and confidence. Self-concept strengthens, and the psychological burden of concealment begins to lift.

Social boundaries do not disappear through resistance alone, but they can be reshaped. Each act of renegotiation challenges rigid norms, expanding the possibilities for inclusion. Change unfolds gradually, through lived example rather than decree. This process also invites communities to reflect. Resistance exposes the cost of exclusion, prompting questions about values, compassion, and responsibility. It reveals that boundaries are not fixed; they are maintained by choice and therefore open to change.

Chapter Six closes with this tension, between boundary and belonging, regulation and resilience. The psychological impact of Christianity on society cannot be understood solely through its structures of control or moments of exclusion. It must also be understood through the human capacity to adapt, resist, and seek wholeness. In this space of negotiation, the possibility of dignity, healing, and reimagined belonging emerges.

Reflective Pause

✓ Social boundaries shape lives quietly and persistently. They influence how people move through the world, how they speak, who they trust, and how they see themselves. For many, these boundaries are learned early and reinforced often, through belief, tradition, and social expectation.

✓ The experiences explored in this chapter reveal that exclusion is rarely sudden. It unfolds through repeated signals of who belongs and who does not, who is affirmed and who is tolerated, who is visible and who must remain hidden. Over time, these signals leave psychological marks that shape identity and emotional life.

✓ This pause invites reflection rather than judgment. It asks the reader to consider how boundaries have operated in their own life, where belonging felt secure, where it felt conditional, and where silence felt safer than honesty. These experiences may be personal or observed by others, but they are rarely absent.

✓ Belief can offer meaning and community, yet it can also become a tool of regulation. Holding these realities together requires honesty. It requires acknowledging that harm can exist alongside good intentions, and that psychological consequences often outlast the rules that produced them.

✓ As you pause here, consider the cost of exclusion and the courage required to resist it. Consider what it means to belong without erasure, and how communities might expand rather than contract their definitions of dignity. These reflections prepare the ground for integrating what this chapter has revealed, not as abstract ideas, but as lived human experience.

CONCLUION

This book began with a simple but demanding question: What has Christianity done to the human mind and to social life? Not in abstraction, and not only in doctrine, but in lived experience, across history, cultures, institutions, and everyday relationships. What has emerged is not a single answer, but a complex portrait of influence that cannot be reduced to praise or critique alone.

Christianity has functioned as a powerful social and psychological force. It has shaped moral frameworks, fostered community, and provided meaning in times of uncertainty and suffering. From the unifying effect of belief to cases of discrimination, the book revealed the multifaceted impact of Christianity on the individual and society in general. It starts with social psychology to reveal the effect of Christian values on personal identity, belonging, and morality. The development of Christianity from a marginal movement to a major force in defining social norms and responsibilities is also discussed. Cases of discrimination even against early Christians are also considered, with their psychological effects on them, which was also linked to our today's church. However, the positive contributions of Christianity to social stability, dignity, and human rights are also discussed in the book .

At the same time, the same belief systems have been entangled with power. As Christianity became institutionalized, it shaped norms, boundaries, and hierarchies that affected who was included and who was excluded, whose identities were affirmed and whose were constrained. These dynamics carried psychological consequences, shaping identity, regulating behavior, and leaving emotional marks that persist long after specific rules or eras have passed. It is important to know that the psychological effects of Christianity are not static but, rather, a dynamic interplay between belief, experiences, and cultures.

Throughout this book, social psychology has served as a lens to understanding these realities. It has helped illuminate how belief becomes internalized, how authority shapes conscience, and how belonging can become conditional. It has shown how shame, stigma, and silence function alongside meaning, care, and moral guidance. These are not contradictions; they are coexisting outcomes of powerful social systems.

The chapters tracing history and cultural encounter revealed that belief rarely operates in isolation. Christianity moved through existing societies, often aligning with political authority and cultural dominance. In these encounters, identity was reshaped, values displaced, and spiritual traditions marginalized. The psychological effects of these processes were not only collective, but deeply personal, experienced in memory, self-concept, and belonging.

The exploration of social boundaries brought these dynamics into sharper focus. Moral regulation around gender, sexuality, and acceptable identity revealed how belief can move from guidance to control. For those who lived at or beyond these boundaries, exclusion carried psychological weight. Yet even within constraint, human agency remained present, expressed through resistance, reinterpretation, and the ongoing search for dignity and wholeness.

This book does not argue for the abandonment of faith, nor does it seek to defend it uncritically. Instead, it invites a more honest engagement with Christianity's psychological and social impact, one that acknowledges both its contributions and its costs. Such honesty is not a threat to belief; it is a condition for maturity, healing, and meaningful dialogue. In this world of ours that craves connection, understanding these dynamics matters because belief continues to shape societies today. Moral frameworks, social norms, and institutional practices carry forward the legacies explored in these pages. Awareness of their psychological effects creates the possibility for more compassionate, inclusive, and reflective engagement moving forward.

If this work has succeeded, it has done so not by resolving tension, but by making it visible. The hope is that readers, whether Christian or not, academic, or not, leave with deeper insight into how belief shapes human life, and with greater care for the minds, identities, and experiences of others. The conversation does not end here. It continues wherever belief meets humanity, and wherever understanding becomes the ground for shared dignity.

CLOSING REFLECTION

This book does not ask readers to abandon belief, nor does it demand agreement. It invites honesty about power, identity, belonging, and the psychological impact of faith on human life. Reflection is not the end of the conversation; it is the beginning.

REFERENCES

Burnes, R. and Stanley, J. 2017. Teaching LGBTQ Psychology. Washington, DC: America. Psychological Association.

Colman. 2014. Marriage, Family, and the Moral Order. Journal of Christian Ethics 32(2): 145–160.

Gaines, S. O., Jr., & Reed, E. S. 1995. Prejudice: From Allport to DuBois. American Psychologist, 50(2), 96-103

Han, S. 2018. Neurocognitive basis of racial ingroup bias in empathy. Trends in Cognitive Sciences, 22(5), 400-421. [PDF] https://www.strategian.com/2020/06/07/the-psychological-origins-of-prejudice-discrimination-and-racism/

McCain, Danny. 2005. Note on New Testament Introduction. Jos, Nigeria: African Christian Textbook (ACTS).

Merker, Matt. 2021. Corporate Worship: How the Church Gathers as God's People. Wheaton, Illinois, USA: Crossway.

Nnaoma Kanu. 2022. Lecture Note on Pauline Epistles. West Africa Theological Seminary. Ipaja, Lagos Nigeria.

Ray Ortlund. 2014. The Gospel: *How the Church Portrays the Beauty of Christ Building Healthy Churches*

Webmaster. 2025. *A Brief History of Discrimination Through Time.* https://www.thewatchtower.com/a-brief-history-of-discrimination-through-time

www.strategian.com/2020/06/07/the-psychological-origins-of-prejudice-discrimination-and-racism/

DISCUSSION GUIDES

This guide is offered as a companion to *The Psychological Impact of Christianity on Society*. It is not intended to test understanding or direct interpretation. Instead, it invites reflection, dialogue, and thoughtful engagement with the ideas explored throughout the book.

Readers may choose to use this guide individually, in classrooms, discussion groups, counseling or ministry settings, or community conversations. Each section is optional. There are no right or wrong answers, only honest inquiry.

Chapter One: Christianity And Social Psychology

Chapter Snapshot

This chapter introduces Christianity as both a belief system and a social-psychological force. It explores how faith shapes behavior, identity, meaning, and social cohesion, and explains why psychology provides a valuable lens for understanding religion's influence on human life.

Key Themes to Sit With

✓ Faith as a social force

- ✓ Identity formation
- ✓ Belonging and cohesion
- ✓ Psychological influence of belief

Reflection Questions

1. In what ways has faith shaped behavior and identity in your own life or community?
2. How do belief systems influence how people understand right and wrong?
3. Where do you see the psychological effects of religion most clearly, in individuals or in society?
4. Can faith shape people even when they do not actively practice it?
5. What does it mean to belong to a belief community?

Chapter Two: Historical And Institutional Development Of Christianity

Chapter Snapshot

This chapter traces Christianity's development from its early beginnings through institutional growth, political involvement, and global expansion. It examines how history shaped authority, norms, and the psychological influence of the church over time.

Key Themes to Sit With

- ✓ Institutional power
- ✓ Authority and legitimacy
- ✓ Religion and politics
- ✓ Historical continuity
- ✓ Psychological influence of institutions

Reflection Questions

1. How does historical context influence how religion is practiced today?
2. In what ways does institutional authority shape belief?
3. Can religious institutions both protect and control communities?
4. How does history continue to shape modern faith experiences?
5. Where do you see tension between spiritual teaching and institutional power?

Chapter Three: Discrimination In The Early Centuries And Its Psychological Implications

Chapter Snapshot

This chapter explores persecution, exclusion, and internal conflict in early Christianity, highlighting how discrimination shaped group identity, resilience, and psychological coping within emerging faith communities.

Key Themes to Sit With

✓ Persecution and identity
✓ Group conflict
✓ Psychological resilience
✓ Social exclusion
✓ Faith under pressure

Reflection Questions

1. How does discrimination shape group identity?

2. What psychological effects emerge when belief is practiced under threat?

3. How do shared struggles strengthen or divide communities?

4. Where do you see parallels between early persecution and modern exclusion?

5. How does suffering influence belief?

Chapter Four: Positive Psychological And Social Contributions

Chapter Snapshot

This chapter examines Christianity's positive influence on social life, including contributions to moral frameworks, education, social stability, family structures, and community cohesion.

Key Themes to Sit With

✓ Moral development
✓ Social stability
✓ Education and progress
✓ Family systems
✓ Meaning and purpose

Reflection Questions

1. What positive social contributions of Christianity stand out to you?

2. How can belief systems promote psychological well-being?
3. Where do moral frameworks support healthy communities?
4. Can religion contribute to social progress without control?
5. How do values shape family and social life?

Chapter Five: Culture, Power, And Identity Formation

Chapter Snapshot

This chapter explores how Christianity interacted with culture through power, leading to displacement, spiritual invalidation, gender hierarchy, and identity fragmentation, particularly in colonized contexts.

Key Themes to Sit With

✓ Cultural encounter
✓ Power and dominance
✓ Identity disruption
✓ Spiritual displacement
✓ Internal conflict

Reflection Questions

1. How does power shape which cultures are valued?
2. What happens psychologically when identity is fragmented?
3. Can belief coexist with cultural continuity?
4. How does spiritual invalidation affect self-worth?
5. Where do you see identity negotiated rather

than inherited?

Chapter Six: Social Boundaries

Chapter Snapshot

This chapter examines how Christianity has shaped social boundaries around morality, gender, sexuality, and belonging. It explores regulation, exclusion, stigma, and the psychological consequences of living within or beyond accepted norms while also highlighting resistance and renegotiation.

Key Themes to Sit With

✓ Moral regulation
✓ Gender roles
✓ Sexual identity
✓ Stigma and shame
✓ Belonging and resistance

Reflection Questions

1. How are social boundaries enforced in subtle ways?
2. What psychological effects emerge when belonging is conditional?
3. How does shame function as a tool of regulation?
4. Where do you see resistance taking quiet forms?
5. What does authentic belonging require?

Group Conversation

i) Which chapter challenged your thinking the most

and why?

ii) Where did you feel tension or discomfort while reading?

iii) What ideas felt affirming, even if difficult?

iv) How might these insights change how communities practice inclusion?

v) What questions are you still holding?

AUTHOR'S NOTE - DR. RUSHAYNE STEWART

This book emerged from years of study, professional practice, and lived experience at the intersection of faith, psychology, and society. My work as a scholar and practitioner has consistently brought me into contact with individuals and communities shaped, both positively and painfully, by belief systems that influence identity, belonging, and emotional well-being.

I approach Christianity neither as a distant observer nor as an unquestioning insider. Instead, I engage it as a powerful social and psychological force, one capable of offering meaning, stability, and hope, while also shaping boundaries that affect dignity, inclusion, and mental health. The aim of this work is not to settle debates, but to illuminate patterns that often go unnamed.

Throughout this book, I have sought to hold complexity with care. Faith has contributed to social good, moral development, and communal resilience. At the same time, it has been intertwined with power structures that have left lasting psychological effects on individuals and cultures. Acknowledging both realities is not an act of rejection, but of honesty.

This book is offered as an invitation to reflect, to question, and to engage thoughtfully with the psychological impact of belief on human life. My hope is that readers, regardless of background or conviction, will find space here for insight, dialogue, and deeper understanding.

CO-AUTHOR'S NOTE - EMMANUEL CHIGBU

Contribution to this book is rooted in a deep interest in how belief systems shape societies, moral imagination, and collective identity. Christianity has played a formative role in social life across cultures, influencing not only spiritual expression but also values, relationships, and structures of authority. Understanding this influence requires careful examination, not assumption.

As a researcher, I am particularly attentive to the ways religion interacts with culture and power. History reveals that belief rarely operates in isolation; it is mediated through institutions, traditions, and social norms that shape how people perceive themselves and others. This book reflects a commitment to examining those dynamics thoughtfully and responsibly.

Collaboration on this work allowed for meaningful dialogue across perspectives. While our voices are distinct, they are united by a shared commitment to intellectual honesty and respect for lived experience. This partnership strengthened the depth and balance of the analysis presented here.

I hope readers approach this book not as a final statement, but as a conversation, one that encourages critical thinking, empathy, and awareness of how belief continues to shape social life in complex ways. If this work prompts reflection and constructive dialogue, it has fulfilled its purpose.

ABOUT THE AUTHOR

Dr. Rushayne Stewart

Dr. Rushayne Stewart is a scholar, counsellor, Christian educator, and global speaker born in Jamaica, currently residing in the United States. Holding double doctorate degrees in Christian Psychology and Counselling and another one in Christian Education. Dr. Stewart brings together the depth of academic knowledge with the heart of a compassionate guide.

For more than two decades, he has served in diverse fields including mental health, social services, veteran care, homelessness support, and community outreach. His work has carried him across continents, where he has spoken in churches, schools, and international conferences-always with one central message: your life has value, your voice matters, and your story is not over.

Dr. Stewart's passion lies in bringing faith and psychology together to offer hope for the brokenhearted, healing for the wounded, and dignity for those who feel forgotten. Drawing on both his professional expertise and his personal conviction, he has dedicated his life to encouraging those in despair, equipping communities to respond with compassion, and reminding the world that even in silence, pain, and scars-there is always light to be found.

ABOUT THE AUTHOR

Emmanuel Chigbu

About the Co- Author

Emmanuel Chigbu is a dedicated Christian educator and emerging leader from Nigeria. Born in Ebute-Metta, Lagos, he hails from Isiala-Ngwa North, Abia State. Emmanuel earned a First-Class Honours degree in Christian Education from West Africa Theological Seminary, Lagos.

As a devoted member of the Redeemed Christian Church of God - The Potter's House, Emmanuel's life is guided by principles of faith, hard work, and service. His interests include singing, teaching, book editing, and writing, with contributions to multiple publications by esteemed authors both locally and internationally.

These passions have inspired Emmanuel in pursuing a Master's degree to enhance his impact on educational development in Nigeria. His commitment to academic excellence and community service underscores his potential as a future leader.